D1567470

HARDWOOD
GLORY

HARDWOOD GLORY

A LIFE OF JOHN WOODEN

BARBARA OLENYIK MORROW

Indiana Historical Society Press | Indianapolis 2014

© 2014 Indiana Historical Society Press

This book is a publication of the
Indiana Historical Society Press
Eugene and Marilyn Glick Indiana History Center
450 West Ohio Street
Indianapolis, Indiana 45202-3269 USA
www.indianahistory.org
Telephone orders 1-800-447-1830
Fax orders 1-317-234-0562
Online orders @ http://shop.indianahistory.org

Library of Congress Cataloging-in-Publication Data

Morrow, Barbara Olenyik.
Hardwood glory : a life of John Wooden / Barbara Olenyik Morrow.
    pages cm
Includes bibliographical references and index.
ISBN 978-0-87195-361-2 (cloth : alk. paper)
1. Wooden, John, 1910-2010. 2. Basketball coaches—United States—Biography. I. Title.
GV884.W66M67 2014
796.323092—dc23
[B]
                    2014020096

To my Morrow men

Contents

Acknowledgments

"Goodness gracious sakes alive!" was an expression Coach John Wooden invoked from time to time, uttered usually when his players did something that displeased him. In researching this book, I also regularly uttered a "goodness" expression, namely, "Thank goodness" that so many people were willing to help me.

I never met Coach Wooden; he died before this project was undertaken. I was fortunate, however, to spend an afternoon with his daughter, Nan, who shared stories about her father, showed me family photos, and gave me a tour of the suburban Los Angeles neighborhood that her father had long called home. She also introduced me to Paul Ma, the owner of VIP's Family Restaurant in Tarzana, California, where for years coach regularly ate breakfast and where, as the walls and shelves testify, Wooden's memory is very much alive.

At the University of California, Los Angeles, I received enormous help from Bill Bennett, special projects and events coordinator for UCLA Athletics. He gave me access to a wealth of material and continued to provide information long after my return to Indiana. Other UCLA staff members also lent assistance, and I especially thank Emily Greer, curator of Coach Wooden's "den" in the UCLA Athletic Hall of Fame; Alex Timiraos, associate director of sports information; and Coach Steve Alford, who agreed to write this book's foreword.

The list of Hoosiers deserving my thanks is long, and I begin by expressing my gratitude to Curtis H. Tomak of Martinsville. I am indebted to him, Joanne Raetz Stuttgen, and Norma J. Tomak for their thorough research on Wooden's Indiana roots—research that appeared in 2012 in the spring/summer and fall/winter issues of *Connections: The Hoosier Genealogist*, a publication of the Indiana Historical Society. I used their research as a springboard for my own digging into Wooden's past, and I regularly consulted Curtis, who offered valuable advice and always helpful suggestions.

Helping me, too, was Kevin J. Walker, who spent an evening sharing stories about his father, Clarence Walker, who played for Wooden at Indiana State Teachers College in the late 1940s. Kevin shared with me the diary that his father kept during the 1947–48 season, a journal that is both personal and revealing.

Kevin Jenison, media relations coordinator for athletics at Indiana State University, patiently answered my many questions pertaining to Wooden's years in Terre Haute. Likewise, I am indebted to Jim Powers, the late Ed Ehlers, and Thomas R. Cassady Sr. for sharing their recollections of Wooden during his years at South Bend Central High School. Thanks also goes to Peter DeKever, a Mishawaka historian; Greg Humnicky, an Indiana Basketball Hall of Fame board member well-versed on high school basketball history in northern Indiana; and Earl Mishler, a compiler of high school basketball records, who helped me verify Wooden's coaching record in South Bend.

Chris May, executive director of the Indiana Basketball Hall of Fame in New Castle, was always accessible and willing to help, as was publications manager Becky Beavers, who tracked down archival photos. Former U.S. Senator Birch Bayh Jr. of Indiana shared information about his father, Birch, who refereed high school state championship games in which Wooden played. I especially enjoyed a story that the former senator relayed about the

UCLA–Purdue University matchup in West Lafayette in 1967. Three Hoosiers with Martinsville ties—Elmer Reynolds, Jerry Sichting, and Sam Alford—deserve thanks for their stories about Wooden and his legacy. Similar thanks go to Jim Calvin and Hal Hossinger, both with Kendallville connections.

Lendy Pridgen of northern Virginia provided me with his recollections of meeting Wooden decades ago at a basketball camp in North Carolina. Sherrill Luke, a former UCLA student body president, talked to me about Wooden's early years on that campus.

Reference librarians are essential to writers, and I am indebted to many. Particularly helpful were Kevin Wadzinski, Saint Joseph County Public Library; Janice Kistler, Morgan County Public Library; Monique Howell, Indiana State Library; and J. Klamm, Kansas City Public Library. To that list I add Donna Moore, Office of the Registrar, Purdue University, and Linda Griffith, library media specialist, Dayton High School in Dayton, Kentucky. Don Liebig assisted me in gaining access to his many fine UCLA basketball photographs.

Sometimes help comes in unexpected ways, and I am grateful to Ellen Grogan, Carolyn Wendt, and Jane Davis for their bit of sleuthing on my behalf. Julia Nixon remains what she has always been—someone to help me at a moment's notice, as she did in this project's late stages.

My gratitude extends to Ray E. Boomhower, senior editor, and Kathleen Breen, editor, at the Indiana Historical Society Press. Both shepherded my manuscript into a final book, and Ray, an exceptionally gifted writer as well as editor, displayed his usual patience and tact in fielding my many questions throughout the course of this work.

Finally, I salute all the friends who cheered me on as I delved deeper into Wooden's life, and I thank my husband, Doug, and my four sons—Matt, Jimmy, Andrew, and Nathan. As a mother who spent years watching her sons play basketball, as a wife who observed her spouse coaching the sport, and as the manager of a home alive with hoops talk and bursting with sneakers, jerseys, basketballs, and other gear, I could not help but come to appreciate the game. My family pointed the way to Coach Wooden, and this book.

Foreword

When I was hired as the head coach at UCLA the final weekend in March 2013, I could not help but think that my career might be coming full circle. I, like so many children growing up in the state of Indiana, was introduced to basketball at a young age. With a father who had been a longtime high school basketball coach in the state, I was very familiar with the roots of John Wooden's career and his accomplishments.

As a first grader, I grew up learning the game and falling in love with it at Martinsville High School. I was born twenty-seven miles from that high school, which Coach Wooden attended in the 1920s before his All-American days as a guard at Purdue University. My dad, Sam, served as Martinsville's high school coach for four years. And I knew that the Martinsville gymnasium had some history, as Coach Wooden had played there decades ago.

I tell people that when you grow up in Indiana, you learn how to play basketball before learning your ABCs or how to count. As a first grader, I was probably the only kid who was picked up by the school bus in one place and dropped off somewhere completely different. But I wanted to be dropped off where my dad was coaching basketball. That was at Glenn Curtis Memorial Gym, the same building in which Coach Wooden had played when he was in high school. I can remember learning the sport as a little guy, getting my start in the game of basketball, where Coach Wooden had been a major presence.

I was ten years old when Coach Wooden in his final year as head coach led the Bruins to the 1975 National Collegiate Athletic

Association Championship, his tenth national title. I remember watching Coach Wooden's team win the title that year, and then the very next year, watching Coach Bob Knight early in his tenure guide Indiana University to the 1976 NCAA Championship. I still consider it very special to have observed these two basketball icons at the end and start of their respective careers.

While I no longer shoot hoops in Coach Wooden's Martinsville gym or watch tapes of him as I did during my first coaching job at Manchester College, I now have the privilege of serving as head coach of the program he made famous. I also have the privilege of being in the place that he called home after leaving Indiana—UCLA. Each morning I walk past his eight-foot-tall statue outside Pauley Pavilion. Every day I see reminders all around campus—on banners and in buildings—of the wise words he shared with his student-athletes.

Today I am the father of three children, including two college-aged sons. Decades ago, while watching my dad's basketball practices, little did I know that my basketball journey would take me from Martinsville's gym to Pauley Pavilion. Like Coach Wooden, I am proud of my Hoosier roots. I am also honored to take the reins of the basketball program he made legendary.

Coach Steve Alford
UCLA
2013

Prologue

"Like most coaches, my program revolved around fundamentals,
conditioning, and teamwork. But I differed radically in several
respects. I never worried about how our opponent would play us,
and I never talked about winning."

It is not often in this modern era that two statues of the same
man are unveiled within six months of each other. Yet that is what
occurred in 2012. In March the bronze likeness of a bent-kneed John
Robert Wooden was unveiled on a street in downtown Indianapolis.
In October, outside a pavilion in Southern California, the public got
its first glimpse of an eight-foot-tall bronze Wooden, depicted with
his arms crossed and a rolled-up game program in hand.

That Wooden's image would be immortalized in both locales is
not surprising. The man who helped define college basketball in
the twentieth century and became an icon of American sports was
both a Hoosier and a Californian. He was born in the small Indiana
town of Martinsville near the start of the last century. His claim to
fame came first as an accomplished athlete, helping his high school
basketball team compete in three state championship games, after
which he earned All-American honors three times in his home state
as a starting guard at Purdue University. After briefly teaching high
school English and coaching several sports in Dayton, Kentucky,
Wooden returned to Indiana. He launched a successful career
coaching basketball at South Bend Central High School and then
joined the college ranks, coaching at Indiana State Teachers College
(now Indiana State University) in Terre Haute.

John Wooden in his iconic pose, including the rolled-up program clutched in his hand. His former player, Kareem Abdul-Jabbar, called Wooden "the consummate teacher."

In 1948, at age thirty-seven, Wooden moved west, as did many Americans in the post–World War II era. He took over the head basketball job at the University of California, Los Angeles, a school with virtually no basketball tradition. He took his family and his coaching skills with him. He also took his midwestern values. For the next six decades he remained in Southern California, creating a basketball dynasty at UCLA and solidifying his place as one of the sporting world's greats. When he died on June 4, 2010, at the Ronald Reagan UCLA Medical Center, he was four months shy of his hundredth birthday.

Wooden's success as a college coach was unprecedented and, in pure numbers, staggering. From 1964 to 1975, he led the UCLA Bruins to ten National Collegiate Athletic Association national basketball championships, including seven in a row—a feat that may never be matched. During that string of championships, he coached the Bruins to four perfect 30–0 seasons, an NCAA men's record that still stands. He also coached UCLA to an eighty-eight-game winning streak, yet another unrivaled men's record. Over the course of his twenty-seven seasons at UCLA, he mentored All-Americans such as Kareem Abdul-Jabbar and Bill Walton, earned the respect of legions of players, and inspired countless would-be roundballers and coaches alike.

These achievements put Wooden in the company of legendary coaches throughout the field of sports. Even in that elite company, he fared especially well. In 2009 *Sporting News* magazine asked more than one hundred coaches and sports experts to name the greatest coach of all time in any sport. Not surprisingly, coaching giants such as the Green Bay Packers' Vince Lombardi, the University of Notre Dame's Knute Rockne, the Boston Celtics's Red

Auerbach, and the New York Yankees' Casey Stengel ranked in the top ten; Wooden stood at number one on the list.

Long before that ranking, however, awards and honors flowed Wooden's way. In 1973 he was inducted into the Naismith Memorial Basketball Hall of Fame as coach, making him the first to be honored as both a player and a coach. (He received the honor as a player in 1960.) In 1977 college basketball's annual player-of-the-year award was named for him. The NCAA bestowed its highest honor, the Theodore Roosevelt award, on Wooden in 1996. And in 2006 the National Collegiate Basketball Hall of Fame in Kansas City, Missouri, honored him as a member of the founding class, along with basketball inventor Doctor James Naismith.

Accolades also poured in from outside the sports world. In 2003 President George W. Bush awarded Wooden the Presidential Medal of Freedom, America's highest civilian honor. Two years later, Indiana bestowed on him its highest honor, the Sachem, an award recognizing a lifetime of excellence and virtue. In earlier decades, entities ranging from service clubs to faith-based organizations to universities rushed to salute not only his accomplishments but also his character.

Celebrated as he was, Wooden never courted celebrity. Raised on a farm and schooled by parents who stressed honesty and hard work, Wooden was strongly influenced by his father. Among the simple maxims he learned at home were: "Don't whine, complain or make excuses," "Be true to yourself," and "Make each day your masterpiece." Wooden drew upon that common-sense advice early in his career and set about crafting his philosophy for winning not just in basketball, but in life. By 1948, before moving to California, he completed his "Pyramid of Success," a teaching and motivational

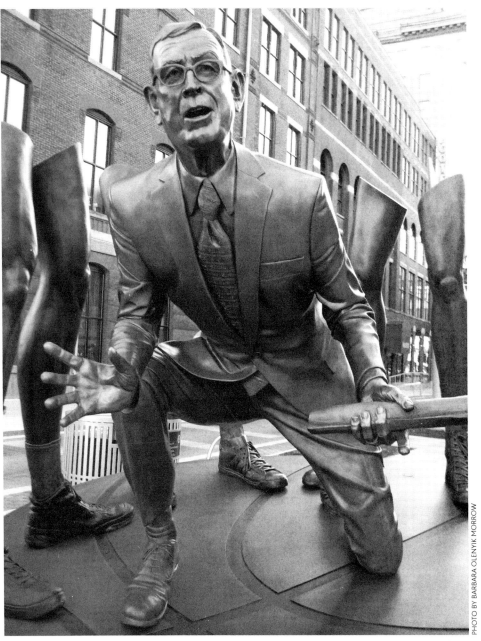

The Wooden's Legacy *sculpture by artist Jeffrey Rouse. Unveiled to the public on March 9, 2012, the sculpture is located just west of the intersection of Georgia and Meridian Streets in Indianapolis.*

tool that outlived him and is studied by not only athletes but also by corporate executives and military officers.

With its emphasis on personal traits such as industriousness, loyalty, and cooperation, Wooden's pyramid pointed to nothing glitzy or showy. The same could be said of the man. Wooden always lived modestly, and even as his teams ruled the college game in the 1970s, his annual compensation (salary plus postgame radio appearances) was never more than $40,500. His appearance and behavior were equally unpretentious. He dressed conservatively in a coat and a tie, abstained from alcohol, and limited his cursing to "Goodness gracious sakes alive." Most notable was his dignity coupled with decency. He reminded players to leave hotel and locker rooms clean on road trips, and he insisted on no excessive celebrating after victories. "You must act like champions," he told his first championship team. "You met some people going up to the top. You will meet the same people going down."

Wooden claimed to enjoy basketball practice sessions more than the actual games because in practices he could instruct. He thought of himself, first and foremost, as a teacher. He stressed preparation, which led him to kick off each season with a footwear lesson—players were shown how to put on their socks and lace up their sneakers to avoid getting play-hampering blisters. He also stressed conditioning, and his teams were always in top physical shape, the result of grueling practices with repetitive drills. Wooden directly supervised the practices, moving up and down the court, demonstrating techniques, calling out the action from meticulously notated three-by-five-inch cards he kept from year to year.

Respected by his players, he was not always loved by them. They sometimes rebelled at his demands, especially his rules for off-court

"When I left UCLA in 1974 and became the highest-paid player in the history of team sports at that time, the quality of my life went down," said Bill Walton. "That's how special it was to have played for John Wooden and UCLA."

conduct. But years later, those same players—having established their careers and raised their own families—expressed appreciation for what the taskmaster taught. Staying in contact and paying homage to Wooden became the norm among those once under his tutelage. As Jamaal Wilkes, a Bruin star in the early 1970s, once explained: "It wasn't until . . . after college, after the NBA [National Basketball Association], when my life focus began to change on marriage, divorce, children, the business world, that I began to sense how special a man he was."

An eight-foot-tall bronze Wooden statue stands guard outside of UCLA's Pauley Pavilion. Sculptor Blair Buswell worked with Wooden's children, Nan and Jim, to get every detail right. "I just wanted people to look at him and be able to say, 'That's John Wooden,'" said Nan.

Referees and opposing coaches also had beefs against Wooden. Intensely competitive, he was known for "riding the refs," though in ways not always apparent to spectators. He would place his signature rolled-up program to his mouth and bark out his complaints. In a like manner, he would also yell at other teams' players, infuriating their coaches and leading him to later reproach himself, saying that was behavior he "may be ashamed of more than anything else."

Throughout his life, Wooden had a loyal and enthusiastic supporter—his wife, Nell, to whom he was equally devoted. High-school sweethearts, they were married for nearly fifty-three years, until Nell's death in 1985. During Wooden's days as a player, they developed a pregame ritual that lasted throughout his career: they made eye contact, Nell gave the thumbs-up sign, and he winked or nodded back. Rarely did Nell miss a game. She rode with him in the family car, with players crammed in the backseat, when he coached in South Bend. Likewise, she traveled with him to every NCAA Final Four tournament, whether or not the Bruins were competing, for nearly forty years. She helped in other ways, too, from washing high school players' socks with her special softener to assuring Wooden he ought not to accept higher-paying jobs outside of coaching.

After Wooden officially retired from basketball in 1975 at age sixty-four, he found his way to a new career. Through lectures he gave and books he wrote, through his sharing of the "Pyramid of Success," through his example of everyday living, he spent his last decades coaching others how to age gracefully and how to bridge generations. Retaining wit and sharpness of mind, he maintained an active schedule well into his nineties, traveling, attending Bruin games, keeping up correspondence, reciting poetry to students, befriending young coaches, and welcoming a steady stream of admirers to his suburban Los Angeles condominium.

When death came, Wooden was mourned throughout the sports world and beyond. President Barack Obama called him "an incredible coach and an even better man." The *Los Angeles Times* wrote in an editorial: "Remembering Wooden as merely a coach is like recalling Abraham Lincoln as just a president. Some men transcend their office." Wooden, always humble, likely would have been embarrassed by any comparison to Lincoln, a leader he so greatly admired. So, too, Wooden likely would have been embarrassed by the hoopla that attended the unveiling of his two statues, and would have thought himself undeserving of such recognition. "He would have been against it. Absolutely. Unless his whole team could be out there," grandson Greg Wooden told a reporter outside UCLA's basketball arena, Pauley Pavilion, the day the commanding bronze monument of Wooden was unsheathed at a public ceremony.

But at the foot of that statue is a plaque, and Wooden likely would have approved of the quote inscribed upon it. The quote is his, the wording hammered out early in his career and then tweaked from time to time, the meaning serving as the credo by which he tried to live his long life: "Success is peace of mind which is a direct result of self-satisfaction in knowing you made the effort to become the best of which you are capable."

1

"It's what you learn after you know it all that counts."

In the first decade of the twentieth century, Americans grew accustomed to headline-grabbing news. In 1901 President William McKinley was shot by an assassin and died eight days later. In 1903 the Wright Brothers soared over Kitty Hawk in the first machine-powered flight. At mid-decade, an earthquake and fire destroyed San Francisco. And in 1909 explorer Robert Peary reached the place that had long captured people's imaginations, the North Pole.

The following year, amid more headline grabbers, a young Hoosier couple savored news of a distinctly personal nature. Inside the *Martinsville Daily Reporter* on October 14, 1910, appeared this brief announcement: "Born to Mr. and Mrs. Hugh Wooden, North Jefferson street, a son—John Robert."

The baby arrived at one o'clock in the morning on that Friday— early enough to make the day's newspaper deadline—and he entered the world with some heft. Birth announcement postcards mailed the next day listed his weight at thirteen pounds. Named for his grandfathers, John was the third child born to Roxie and Hugh Wooden. Already at home was a brother, Maurice, older than John by three years, and a sister, Harriett Cordelia, a year older.

John barely got to know his sister. She died from diphtheria in 1913, a few months shy of her fourth birthday. The family's heartbreak was compounded when another child, a girl, died at birth

IHS, JAY SMALL POSTCARD COLLECTION, P. 391

Completed in 1859, the Morgan County Courthouse in Martinsville is one of the few pre-Civil War courthouses still standing in Indiana. The Italianate-style courthouse was designed by architect Isaac Hodgson and constructed by Perry Blankenship.

that same year. "I doubt if Mother ever really recovered from the deaths of her two little girls," John wrote years later. Still, the Wooden family continued to expand and John eventually had two more brothers—Daniel, born in 1917, and William, in 1922.

At the time of John's birth, his parents were relative newcomers to Martinsville, a typical small midwestern town with a pre-Civil War courthouse marking it as the seat of government for Morgan County. Indianapolis, the state capital that within a year hosted its first 500-mile race, sat thirty miles to the north.

Twenty miles to the south, through increasingly hilly, heavily forested terrain, sat another sleepy courthouse town, Bloomington, home to Indiana University.

Both of John's parents were Morgan County natives. Roxie Anna was from Centerton, a small community just north of Martinsville. Her father, John H. Rothrock Sr., was a farmer and grain elevator businessman with ties to the area dating back to 1866. Several miles west of Centerton was the crossroads hamlet of Hall. Hugh, whose full name was Joshua Hugh Wooden, was raised on a farm near there, his forebears having come north from Kentucky in the 1850s. Hugh's father, Robert, both farmed and taught school.

A 2014 photograph of the former Wooden family home at 460 North Jefferson Street in Martinsville. The family lived here from 1907 to 1914, and it is believed to be the birthplace of Maurice, Harriett Cordelia, John, and their unnamed sister.

PHOTO BY BARBARA OLENYIK MORROW, COURTESY HERBERT A. AND FLORENCE YVONNE KNIEPER

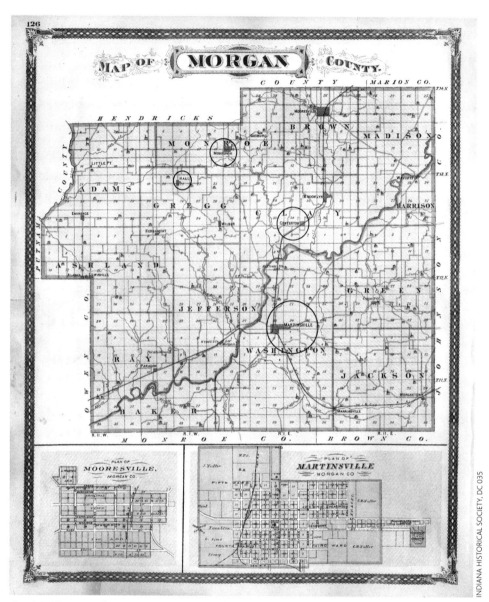

An 1876 map of Morgan County, Indiana, including detailed city maps for Mooresville and Martinsville. Created in 1821, the county was named for American Revolutionary War hero Daniel Morgan.

In April 1905 Hugh and Roxie married. He was twenty-three years old, and she was seventeen. They lived first in Hall, moved two years later to nearby Martinsville, and eventually settled into a modest home at 460 North Jefferson Street. It was there that John was born.

If John had any memories of his early years in Martinsville, he did not record them. For much of his life he apparently believed his birthplace was in his father's home village: "My roots are deep in Indiana soil, for on October 14, 1910, I was born in a little place called Hall," he wrote in his 1972 book *They Call Me Coach*. John did live in Hall briefly; his parents left Martinsville and moved the family there in September 1914, when John was almost four. A year later, in September 1915, the Woodens moved again to the nearby town of Monrovia. It was in that Morgan County community, as John said later, "that my earliest memories came into focus."

Hugh worked a small farm in Monrovia. He also delivered mail throughout the countryside and sometimes permitted John, known as John Bob in his youth, to tag along on the route. John enjoyed his father's attention; even better, he loved riding in the horse-drawn buggy. "I had but one dream, to own a buggy with red wheels and a little black mare to pull it," he recalled. His cousin owned such a rig, and John thrilled at opportunities to take over the reins and head to White Lick, a stream of the White River that bisected the county. "I'd drive it out on a gravel bar and wash and shine it until it sparkled," he said. Of time spent in Monrovia, John added: "Between the mail route and our small farm I thought we had a wonderful life."

In March 1917 the Woodens moved yet again, this time to a fifty-eight-acre farm near Centerton that Roxie inherited from her father. Hugh planted the fields in wheat, corn, alfalfa, and potatoes, and

Roxie tended to the simple white farmhouse that had no electricity and consisted of two bedrooms, a sparsely furnished living room, and a kitchen heated by a wood-burning stove. Nearby was a barn, a smokehouse for curing meat, and a well where water was pumped by hand. An outhouse (a three-holer) sat some distance away.

Hugh expected his sons to help with chores, and John's duties included milking the family's cows and cleaning out barn stalls. The family garden—planted in peas, carrots, squash, and beans—was bigger than the house, and Roxie put young John to work hoeing, pulling weeds, and removing worms from tomatoes. She also sent John and his brothers to hunt wild berries that Roxie made into jellies and jams. "We'd pick the fruit, help cut it up, and then seal the jars," John said, recalling his kitchen duties. The work had its rewards; John especially loved his mother's persimmon pudding and peach cobbler.

A 2014 photograph of the Centerton home where the Wooden family moved in March 1917. The house formerly had only four rooms and no front porch.

Proud of each of her children, Roxie took pains to appreciate them equally. "Our value to her was because of who we were, not what we did," John said. If he or one of his brothers received a special honor, John recalled how Roxie would "dedicate a little extra attention to the other ones to make sure we understood that her love had nothing to do with our accomplishments." Despite the death of her two daughters and the heavy demands of farm life, Roxie never wallowed in self-pity. Nor did she complain about sacrifices made, such as wearing ill-fitting shoes donated by others so she would have money for necessities for her children. "When I think of mother," John said years later, "I think of hard work: cooking, canning, mending, washing on the washboard, churning our own butter. I think of perseverance."

Like Roxie, Hugh did not shirk hard work, and years of physical labor had made him strong enough to, as John put it, "bend a thick iron bar with his bare hands." Equal to Hugh's strength was his gentleness, evident in countless ways. John recalled the time at a local gravel pit when he and his father saw a man whipping a team of horses struggling under a heavy load. Hugh stepped up to the team, spoke quietly to the horses, grasped the bridle, and calmly led them forward. "It was an incredible reminder that gentleness can fix in a moment what an hour of shouting fails to achieve," noted John.

As humble as he was compassionate, Hugh taught his sons to treat everyone with respect. "It didn't matter if they were rich or poor, well dressed or in dirty work clothes," John said. "My father . . . spoke with the same quiet tone, the same level of interest, and the same genuine concern in every conversation he had." Hugh also advised his sons to strike the right balance between pride and humility: "'Remember this,' he used to say to us. 'You're as good as anybody. But never forget you're no better than anybody, either.'"

Hugh's kindly disposition notwithstanding, John recalled getting one "real licking" from his father. He and his brother Maurice, nicknamed Cat, were cleaning out horse stalls one morning when Maurice tossed a pitchfork of manure into John's face. Furious, John charged at his brother and cursed at him. Hearing the ruckus, Hugh stepped between the boys, listened to both sides of the story, and then disciplined them both. "Dad certainly didn't condone what Cat had done, but neither would he put up with my loss of control or swearing," John said. That incident, along with the fact that he never heard his father use profanity, taught John to temper his tongue throughout his life, with his sharpest curse being no curse at all: "When I get mad, the strongest thing I can say is 'goodness gracious sakes alive.'"

Upon reaching school age, John attended most, if not all, of first grade in Monrovia. But with the move to the new farm, he and Maurice transferred to Centerton Grade School, a two-story brick schoolhouse down the road from their home. In the evenings by the light of a coal-oil lamp, Hugh supplemented his sons' classroom instruction. Some nights he read aloud from the plays of William Shakespeare; other nights he read poetry, everything from Edgar Allan Poe's "The Raven" to Alfred, Lord Tennyson's *Idylls of the King*. He always closed with a verse or two from the Bible, though on bitter cold nights, he did more: Hugh placed heated bricks wrapped in towels at the foot of the boys' beds to keep them warm.

While farm chores and studying took priority in the Wooden household, Hugh understood the importance of play. Throughout America, baseball reigned as the national pastime, and Hugh, a decent pitcher, though his first love was checkers, leveled off a field and made a ball diamond behind the barn. The field was crude, it lacked a backstop, and John and his brothers had to whittle their own bats from tree limbs. But John had a strong arm, and by the time he was thirteen or fourteen, he played with older boys on Centerton's town team. The family ball diamond was not retired, however. Youth from neighboring towns dropped by for weekend games, one being Emmett "Branch" McCracken, a talented athlete from Monrovia who was older than John by two years. The paths of John and Branch, who later played and coached basketball at Indiana University, often crossed over the years.

Basketball, a game invented barely twenty years before John was born, may not have been America's favorite pastime, but the new sport was exploding in popularity in Indiana. It fit perfectly in the landscape of small Hoosier towns and farm communities, where tiny high schools could not afford or field enough players for football or baseball teams. Basketball also fit the mood of rural Indiana, providing families with a welcome diversion between fall harvest and spring planting. More importantly perhaps, basketball united Hoosier farm families, allowing them to bond with their school team and showcase civic pride.

At the Wooden farm, Hugh did what many fathers of that era did. Around the time John turned eight, Hugh knocked the bottom out of an old tomato basket and nailed it to the hayloft in the barn, while Roxie stuffed old rags into her black cotton hose to make a basketball. On many an evening, with their chores completed, John and Maurice squared off, dribbling and darting, shoving and shooting. They reveled in the fun of spirited games in a state gone thoroughly, and hopelessly, "basketball crazy."

2

"Never mistake activity for accomplishment."

In 1920, when John Wooden turned ten, America entered what many considered a crazy decade—the Roaring Twenties. The Great War in Europe had just ended, and war-weary Americans were in a partying mood, eager for excitement and ready to celebrate colorful characters. Among the sports heroes Americans embraced were baseball slugger Babe Ruth, heavyweight boxing champion Jack Dempsey, a three-year-old colt named Man o' War, and two men who became football legends—Chicago Bears halfback Harold "Red" Grange and University of Notre Dame coach Knute Rockne.

The extent to which John idolized, or even paid attention to, the mythmaking athletes of the 1920s is not clear. But he did pay attention to Earl W. Warriner. A returning war veteran, Warriner was a feisty boxer, an above-average baseball player, and, most important, from John's perspective, coach of the Centerton School basketball team. He was also the school's principal, known by students as strict but fair. "When he gave it to you, you had it coming," John recalled. "On those occasions he'd walk outside and cut a switch from the hedge, trim off its thorns with his silver pocketknife, and then let you have it across the backside a few times. It stung even though I always wore heavy denim overalls."

Because Warriner believed in education before sports, he proceeded cautiously before inviting boys to join Centerton's basketball team. "He allowed no boy to practice or play without specific permission from teachers. Schoolwork had to be completed and classes attended," John said. Parents also had to give permission, which Hugh Wooden did. At age eleven, John was cleared to join the squad.

The grade-school team consisted of eight or nine boys, the number depending on how quickly the fall harvest proceeded. The basketball court, next to the schoolhouse, was dirt, and John and his teammates had to rake away branches, leaves, and sticks before games. Sometimes snow fell, but play continued anyway. Interruptions resulted when the leather ball became lopsided. "As it gradually lost air, we'd unlace it and use a shoehorn to pry the bladder's air tube out, put it between our lips and blow hard," John said. "Unfortunately, it got out-of-round easily."

Playing with a lopsided ball on a potholed dirt court had benefits; John learned to hone his dribbling skills. Playing under the knowledgeable Warriner also had benefits, though sometimes coach's instruction was unwelcome. One day, when John was around thirteen years old, Warriner taught him a hard lesson.

As Centerton's top scorer at the time, John did not lack confidence and admitted he was "probably cocky." On the morning of a big game, players learned that the contest had to be canceled because the truck that transported the opposing team was broken. At noon as usual, John walked home for lunch and returned to school without his basketball jersey, a homemade bib worn over his shirt. But plans changed. The truck was fixed, and the game was back on for 2:00 p.m.

Upon informing Warriner that his jersey was at home, John assumed coach would give him special treatment, either by allowing

Born in Canada, Doctor James Naismith invented the game of basketball late in 1891 while teaching at the Young Men's Christian Association Training School in Springfield, Massachusetts. From 1917 to 1937, he served as a physical education professor at the University of Kansas.

him to play without it or by sending one of the other players to the Wooden farm to fetch it. Instead, Warriner removed John from the starting lineup and made him sit on the bench. There John sat, miserable, as his outmatched team fell behind and lost the game. It was only later, as he reflected on the experience, that John realized Warriner was teaching him that "no player is bigger or better than the team" and that some things were more important than winning. "Maybe I did need to be taken down a notch or two," John said. "The life lessons in responsibility and humility that I needed to learn trumped a hatch mark in the loss column of a grade school-league record book."

Hugh did not try to outcoach Warriner. Neither did he offer much in the way of basketball instruction or attend many games. Rather, Hugh continued to urge his sons to live by what he called "two sets of threes." The first set focused on honesty: "Never lie. Never cheat. Never steal." The second focused on dealing with adversity: "Don't whine. Don't complain. Don't make excuses." "His priorities were different," John said of his father. While family and education were all-important, Hugh attached little significance to acquiring material possessions, seeking public recognition or, in John's words, "outscoring someone in a basketball game."

In the spring of 1924 John graduated from Centerton. In those days students in rural America did not automatically attend high school, and eighth-grade graduation was usually marked by a ceremony, an event for which John, having earlier passed his examinations with high marks, dressed in clean overalls. He expected no gift, as money remained scarce in the Wooden home, but his father surprised him with a two-dollar bill. Hugh also handed over a crisp, white card, with a favorite poem printed on one side, and a list of seven rules on the other. The rules, which Hugh called his seven-point creed, were:

1. Be true to yourself.
2. Help others.
3. Make each day your masterpiece.
4. Drink deeply from good books, especially the Bible.
5. Make friendship a fine art.
6. Build a shelter against a rainy day.
7. Pray for guidance, and count and give thanks for your blessings every day.

John later acknowledged that his youthfulness prevented him from wholly appreciating the gift's value: "I didn't fully understand how profound Dad's seven-point creed was." Even so, he always kept the handwritten card in his wallet, and when it was finally too crinkled and worn, he made copies that he continued to carry with him. "It was so much more than just a simple present," John wrote later, by then having recognized its importance. "My father gave me the gift of advice."

With Centerton having no school for upper grades, John did in the fall of 1924 what Maurice had done three years earlier—he enrolled in Martinsville High School, seven miles south. The brothers traveled the distance by interurban, an electric-powered rail transportation system that connected Indiana's cities and towns in the early 1900s. Similar to city streetcars, interurban cars sped cross-country at up to sixty miles per hour—a seemingly lightning speed compared to traveling town to town on horseback or in a horse-drawn wagon. John and

A vast network of interurban railroads crisscrossed Indiana, as highlighted in the 1910 Central Electric Railway Association map. Also pictured is the crew for the interurban line that ran from Muncie to New Castle, which operated until 1941.

Maurice boarded the interurban in front of Breedlove's General Store in Centerton each morning and hopped off at the terminal in Martinsville.

At the time of John's enrollment, Martinsville High School had just established itself as a basketball powerhouse and, to many throughout the Hoosier countryside, a basketball mecca. The previous March the high school's team under Coach Glenn Curtis won the 1924 state basketball championship. Just weeks before that, the community celebrated the opening of a new brick-and-limestone gymnasium that could accommodate 5,200 spectators, several hundred more than the town's population. The monstrous hoops hall was declared by a state athletic official to be the largest gym in the state, even bigger than those on the campuses of Indiana and Purdue Universities. "The court was polished hardwood, modern bright lights hung from the ceiling, and the ball was perfectly round," John recalled.

John played on the reserve squad as a freshman, but finances, more than basketball, likely occupied discussions at home. Hugh had long struggled to make a decent living for his family, and in 1919 he had even sold farm animals and equipment at public auction with the intent of moving everyone to Florida. But Roxie's ill health that year thwarted the move, and Hugh resumed farming, though with limited success. Around the time John entered high school, Hugh decided to raise hogs and turned to a bank for help. He borrowed money to buy the animals, the feed on which to fatten them, and the vaccine required to protect them against cholera. But the vaccination serum was bad; all the hogs died. "In those days there was no insurance for this kind of trouble, so we lost everything," John recalled. "Those were very hard times for our family."

Those hard financial times played out against a backdrop of unsettling times across a swath of America. The Ku Klux Klan, a white supremacist group born in the aftermath of the Civil War, experienced a resurgence in the early 1920s, and the revived Klan targeted not just African Americans as "undesirable" but also Roman Catholics, Jews, and immigrants, among others. In Indiana, where Protestantism flourished, patriotism ran high, and racial and ethnic prejudice were accepted, Klan gatherings and parades became common in towns and cities, and cross burnings were known to take place in country fields. By the mid-1920s, between a quarter and a third of all native-born, white males in Indiana belonged to the fast-growing organization. In John's home county alone, upward to 1,600 men claimed Klan affiliation—many of them no doubt attending a Klan rally in Martinsville in October 1923 that attracted "thousands of people," according to a local newspaper.

D. C. Stephenson came to Indiana in 1920, joined the Ku Klux Klan, and became Grand Dragon of the Indiana Realm in 1923. His rise to power crashed to earth in 1925 when he was convicted of the murder of Madge Oberholtzer.

How much John, then in his early teens, was aware of white-robed Klan activities and Klan-sponsored bigotry is not clear. But the message he continually heard at home from his father, "You're as good as anybody. But never

forget you're no better than anybody, either," appeared to have
impressed him more deeply. He was raised not to judge people by
skin color, and as an adult he was forward thinking on race issues.

Meanwhile, farm life for the Woodens and Klan dominance
in Indiana was soon a thing of the past. In the spring of John's
freshman year, Indianapolis-based Klan leader David Curtis
Stephenson—who once publicly boasted, "I am the law in
Indiana!"—was arrested for brutally raping a young woman who
died as a result of the assault. When details became public at

*A 2014 photograph of the house at 410 East Pike Street in Martinsville. Hugh
Wooden and his family moved into this house from their Centerton farm in
1925 and lived there until 1927.*

Stephenson's sensational trial for murder, Hoosiers turned against the Klan's so-called Grand Dragon, and they began abandoning the organization in droves following his November 1925 conviction. By decade's end, the Klan ceased to be a political force in Indiana.

Ceasing for John were his commutes to high school. His freshman year over, he and his family moved to Martinsville in September 1925, settling in a home at 410 East Pike Street. Financial pressures had led Hugh to quit farming for good, and though he and Roxie owned the farm until 1930, the family did not return there to live. The Woodens became permanent townsfolk, and Maurice, heading off that same September to begin his studies at nearby Franklin College, also assumed "townie" status.

As for the Martinsville High School basketball team, it had failed to repeat as state champs in March 1925. Like any loyal fan, John hoped the title would be recaptured in his sophomore year, and he eagerly awaited the upcoming season. Anticipating his move up to varsity, John longed to give Coach Curtis a hand—his long-practicing dribbling hand.

3

"Don't let making a living prevent you from making a life."

When choosing the name "Artesians" for the high school basketball team, Martinsville residents had only to look to the city's history. In 1887 workers drilled a well on the city's west side and, instead of finding the hoped-for gas or oil, discovered a spring from which mineral-rich "artesian" waters bubbled. The property owner, Sylvanus Barnard, was not altogether disappointed. He built a health spa, or sanitarium, at the site in 1888, hoping to cash in on the then-popular belief that the waters possessed healing properties.

The Colonial Sanitarium was one of many in Martinsville, Indiana, that catered to those wishing to partake of the area's healing waters.

Other businessmen drilled and built, and within a decade Martinsville boasted six sanitariums, that number eventually doubling. While many began as cottage-style bathhouses, they quickly evolved into resorts offering services ranging from physical therapy to nutrition counseling. Two Indiana communities farther south, French Lick and West Baden Springs, showcased their mineral waters at luxurious, top-dollar resorts frequented by guests famous and infamous. Martinsville's spas were not as opulent as those downstate, but the community successfully promoted its "healing" waters, and sanitarium guests ranged from working-class midwesterners to rich sophisticates from scattered cities.

Martinsville's largest and most popular spa was the Home Lawn Sanitarium. Located on East Washington Street in the town's most fashionable neighborhood, Home Lawn was where Hugh Wooden

A view of the terraced garden at the Highland Sanitarium in Martinsville. The sanitarium offered mineral baths as a cure for rheumatism.

The North Parlor at the Martinsville Sanitarium.

found employment after leaving the farm and where his duties as bathhouse attendant included giving rubdowns and massages. The spa's guests, many seeking relief from arthritis and other afflictions, often tipped him for his services, and Roxie Wooden carefully recorded the amount each day on a kitchen wall calendar. Even with a salary and tips, however, money was never abundant in the Wooden home. Only "in a great while," John recalled, would Hugh treat the family to dinner at Riley's Café on the courthouse square: "Little did I realize then what an expense one of those dinners was to mom and dad."

Unable to remove themselves completely from farm life, the Woodens planted a garden and continued growing their own vegetables. Likewise, Roxie continued canning and jam making. But John and his brothers did not miss their former chores, and town living offered country boys like themselves ample diversions. As much as anything, John loved being close to the high school and experiencing the excitement that overtook the community when basketball season began. "They used to say when a game was on in Martinsville, 'Don't try to buy anything because everyone's at the game,'" John recalled.

Despite his high hopes, the 1925–26 basketball season began poorly for John, very poorly. He got into a fight with one of the

starters, who, John claimed, used "dirty" tactics: "We went at it hard until Coach [Glenn] Curtis came over, broke up the fight, and told me to apologize for starting it." Believing the other player had intentionally tripped him, John refused to apologize. His anger grew until "finally, I got so worked up that I ripped off my jersey; took off my shoes, socks, and trunks; and threw them down in front of Coach Curtis. Then I stalked off the court."

Years later, when writing about the incident, John said he stayed away for two weeks. In another recollection, he

Closeup of Wooden from a photograph of the Martinsville High School basketball team, 1926.

A contemporary photograph of the entrance to the gymnasium at the former Martinsville High School.

said his absence lasted only a few days. Whatever the time frame, Curtis suggested to John that they forget about what happened and urged him to return to practice. "Of course, I was more than eager to forget about it," said John. "Like all good coaches, [Curtis] understood people very well."

Curtis also understood the game of basketball. In his first year as head coach, the Morgan County native led a team from Lebanon, Indiana, to the 1918 state high school championship. Two seasons later, Curtis took over at Martinsville High School, where he became one of the most successful basketball coaches in the school's history and where the gym was eventually named after him. In 1964 he was inducted into the Indiana Basketball Hall of Fame, one of the first coaches given that honor.

Like Coach Earl W. Warriner at Centerton, Curtis viewed himself as an educator, his mission to teach basketball fundamentals. Before allowing players to come together as a team, he insisted that each first perfect basic skills such as passing, defending, and rebounding. "We drilled. And we drilled. And we drilled. We practiced everything until it was second nature to us," recalled John. Curtis also insisted that his players think about how the game should be played, an insistence that meant the Artesians, as John put it, "may have spent more time practicing without the basketball than with it." In spite of the rocky start to their relationship, John came to highly regard Curtis, who nicknamed him "Pert" for "impertinent," perhaps due to the practice scuffle. John also admired his coach for a decidedly nonathletic reason: Curtis quoted poetry.

Sometimes Curtis recited poems at practices to illustrate a point. Other times he recited bits of inspirational verse before a game or at halftime. Like many sports-loving Americans in the 1920s, Curtis looked to one of the nation's leading sportswriters, Grantland Rice, for language both expressive and motivational. Rice often penned verse within his columns and is known for an oft-quoted stanza: "For when the one Great Scorer comes to write against your name, He marks—not that you won or lost—but how you played the game." That stanza, thanks to Curtis's recitations, became one of John's favorites. As much as any particular poem, however, John liked how Curtis appreciated the art form often heard in the Wooden home, with Hugh in a chair reciting to his

Inducted into the Indiana Basketball Hall of Fame in 1964, Glenn Curtis, Wooden's coach at Martinsville High School, never had a losing season during his nearly twenty years at the school.

sons. As John wrote years later, "I have always been a lover of poetry, and I believe this influenced me to accept [coach]."

Among the rules Curtis expected players to follow during basketball season was "no dating." John might have found the rule easy to obey had it not been for Nellie Riley, who was a year younger. John had first seen her during his freshman year and later at a summer carnival—enough time to think her "cute," though he doubted she had noticed him. But Nellie had noticed, and on a scorching July day she persuaded her best friend's brother to drive her to the Wooden farm, John and his family not having moved yet to town. When Nellie arrived, she waved to John as he plowed a cornfield. Embarrassed by his grimy appearance, he pretended not to see Nellie and started plowing in the opposite direction. Eventually, Nellie left, but when school started in the fall, she confronted him on why he had been so rude. "I hemmed and hawed a little bit, but then told the truth, 'I was all dirty and sweaty,' I said. 'I thought you'd probably make fun of me.'" When Nellie said she would never do that, John recalled that "something happened in me right then—that spark that has never gone away."

The two began spending time together, walking to and from school, visiting Shireman's Ice Cream Parlor on Saturdays, and attending movies featuring reigning Hollywood stars such as Charlie Chaplin and Tom Mix. "When I didn't have twenty cents for tickets, I'd run ahead to the box office and ask the ticket taker, 'Could I pay you later?' In those days you could do that," John said. Those activities aside, the couple mostly sat on the swing on the Rileys' front porch, holding hands and talking.

The location of Nellie's home on South Wayne Street proved troublesome for John. Curtis lived close enough that he could see

JULIUS J. ELLIS

Varsity B. B. 4;
Hi-Y 2, 3, 4;
Hi-Y President 5;
Glee Club 3, 4;
Band Drum Major 2;
Red and Blue Staff 5;
Commercial Club 4;
Latin Club 1, 2, 3.
Jude's enthusiasm sometimes runs away with him, but he is a good sport. We've all kinds of faith in him.

ROSE ELLEN STIERWALT

Sunshine Society 4;
Latin Club 4.
Rose Ellen is Gene's long lost, but newly found pal. She's taking harmony and gets along harmoniously. Being really fond of music she takes in all the operas and such. We see her in the future as a music supervisor—personally we wouldn't mind to learn the charms of music under her tutelage.

RAY RICHARDSON

Debating 4;
"Purple Towers" 4;
Glee Club 4;
Hi-Y 2, 3, 4;
Dramatic Club 3, 4;
Science Club 3;
Math Club 4.
"Thy everlasting yawns in class, confess the pains of idleness." He's the original hard boiled guy, but withal a really remarkable fellow.

NELLIE RILEY

Dramatic Club 3, 4;
Sunshine Society 2, 3, 4;
Uke Club 3, 4;
Glee Club 2, 3, 4;
"Golden Days" 3;
"It Happened In June" 3;
Band 2, 3;
Operetta 2, 3, 4;
Latin Club 1, 2.
With this regular little Irish colleen hearts are trumps. She has a roguish smile and is "cute" to the nth degree.

MARGARET LEAKE

Latin Club 1, 2, 3, 4;
Sunshine Society 2, 3, 4;
Uke Club 4;
Dramatic Club 4;
Glee Club 4;
Operetta 4;
Fall Carnival 1.
Although one can scarcely imagine Margaret — graceful, gracious, and genteel—at a typewriter, we are here to say that looks are often deceiving.

MALCOLM LIND

Latin Club 1, 2, 3, 4;
Math Club 3, 4.
Not exactly a bud, but not quite in full bloom. He talked gravely and walked gravely, and worked gravely, and thought gravely. His studious ways will carry him far.

MARY E. WHITAKER

Dramatic Club 3, 4;
Latin Club 3, 4;
Girl Reserves 3, 4;
Sunshine Society 2, 3, 4;
Glee Club 1;
4H Club 3.
Latin is her favorite subject. Her notebooks have been works of art. Something of hers is always being displayed in Miss Hart's room.

WM. SCHOOLCRAFT

A sturdy son of toil. Bill is one of the youths who collaborate with Mr. Ennis in trying to keep our building so clean. We're here to say this is no mean job with so many of us careless kids about. In the classroom. he both knows and likes chemistry.

Thirty-one

Nellie Riley's senior picture (lower left) from the 1929 Martinsville High School yearbook, The Artesian.

"Robina In Search Of A Husband" Class Play '27.

Hot Dog.

Pains.

At Franklin.

"Pert"

Call The Parson.

Kate And ?

Prexy.

Page from The Artesian *yearbook of Martinsville High School in 1928.
Wooden, nicknamed "Pert," is shown as a young boy on a mule.*

inside the Rileys' kitchen from his dining room window. "During the entire basketball season, Nellie and I made very sure we stayed out" of the kitchen, John said, admitting that he, like his teammates, sometimes skirted Curtis's no-dating rule.

Possessing what her school yearbook described as a "roguish smile," the Irish-bred Nellie was a joiner. She belonged to numerous clubs, including the school pep band, where her cornet-playing skills, unlike her skills in the Girls Ukulele Band, were suspect. Her friends alleged she put the brass instrument to her lips and merely pretended to blow. Still, by joining the pep band Nellie was allowed to sit in the front row at basketball games, and it was from her courtside seat that she and her new "sweetheart" began a little ritual. As Curtis gathered the team in a huddle before each game, John stood so he could see Nellie: "When we made eye contact she'd give me a little thumbs-up, and I'd wink or nod back at her."

John's sophomore year provided ample opportunity for the couple to perfect their ritual. Although not a varsity starter, John was a reliable substitute who helped the Artesians compile a winning regular-season record and knock off opponents in the early stages of the state tournament. In those days, schools of all sizes competed to advance to the championship, with the smallest schools having the opportunity to upset larger ones. That year, 1926, a record 719 Indiana high schools entered the multiweek tournament, up ninefold from a dozen years earlier and evidence of basketball's ever-increasing popularity in the Hoosier State.

The tournament finals were to be played in mid-March in the enormous Exposition Building at the state fairgrounds in Indianapolis. The steel-and-brick structure with banks of windows served as the cattle pavilion for the Indiana State Fair. A year earlier, in 1925, the "Cow Barn," as the building was nicknamed, hosted its first state finals. None other than the founder of basketball, the aging James Naismith, had been a tournament guest. "The possibilities of basketball as seen there were a revelation to me," Naismith wrote of his visit, during which he presented the trophies. "The striking features were the grade of basketball, the splendid spirit of the players and the unbounded enthusiasm of the 15,000 spectators who crowded the Exposition Building. Many were being turned away for a lack of room."

Much to John's delight, the Artesians advanced all the way to the 1926 tourney finals, arriving in Indianapolis as one of sixteen teams hoping to be crowned as state champion. The tournament covered two days, and when the Artesians drew the last game on Friday night, John knew he and his teammates would face a severe physical test. To snare the state title, they would have to win four games in a twenty-five-hour period: the late game Friday, another on Saturday morning, yet another that afternoon, and

PHOTO BY INDIANA HIGH SCHOOL ATHLETIC ASSOCIATION, COURTESY PETER DE KEVER

The Exposition Building, constructed as a cattle pavilion for the Indiana State Fair, hosted the state high school basketball finals in 1925, 1926, and 1927.

Marion High School basketball star Charles "Stretch" Murphy. He later earned All-American honors three times while playing for Purdue University. He was named as a member of the Indiana Basketball Hall of Fame and the Naismith Memorial Basketball Hall of Fame.

COURTESY INDIANA BASKETBALL HALL OF FAME

the championship game on Saturday night. "It was my first experience with competition at that level and intensity," John said. "Most of the 1926 tournament was a blur."

The Artesians handily beat Summitville 50–24 in the first round. Then on Saturday, with the atmosphere inside the Cow Barn every bit as electrifying as Naismith had described the year before, Martinsville squeaked out wins over Logansport (24–20) and then Bedford (28–25). That set the stage for the final matchup, with Martinsville squaring off against the Marion Giants.

Coached by the athletic Gene Thomas, a four-sport letterman at Indiana University, Marion had clobbered Martinsville by a score of 47–32 earlier in the season. The Giants were in search of their first-ever boys' basketball championship, and they hoped that their center, six-foot-six-inch Charles "Stretch" Murphy, would help them achieve their goal. Considered mammoth for players of that era, Murphy later starred at Purdue University and then played professional basketball.

Meanwhile, as tipoff approached for Saturday night's title game, Curtis knew he needed a game plan to throttle big-man Murphy. Nicknamed the "Ol' Fox," Curtis seized on an idea. He had John, nearly a foot shorter than Murphy, do something he never did—jump center. "My job this time was to force as tight a jump as possible so our center could block off against Murphy," John said. The Artesians battled as best they could, helped by John's talented teammate Lester Reynolds. Even so, the Giants prevailed, beating the Artesians 30–23 and carrying off the trophy. Of Curtis's plan, John later said: "The theory may have been correct but Murphy was too much."

Still, the chance to compete in a final game was not lost on John. At age fifteen he had just experienced Hoosier Hysteria in its most glorified form. With hard work and some luck, he aimed to experience it again.

4

"Nothing will work unless you do."

When not dribbling a basketball, doing homework, or courting Nellie Riley, John Wooden spent a good part of his teenage years trying to earn money. Hustling jobs was, in his words, "a never ending task." On Saturdays he often boxed groceries. On Tuesday nights he worked at the Martinsville Elks Club, where he and a fellow employee served the meal, washed dishes, and cleaned the kitchen. Dependent on tips for their earnings, the two always passed the tip tray first to the most generous Elks member, hoping others might take the hint and toss in more than a nickel or a dime.

Summers meant more job hustling. Wooden packed tomatoes and peas in a canning factory, hauled gravel for a crew resurfacing county roads, planted high-tension-line poles into Indiana limestone, and unloaded eighty-five-pound cans of milk on the receiving dock at the Collier Brothers' Creamery. In the afternoons at Collier's, he worked on the bottling line or in the ice-cream plant, wrapping Eskimo Pies in bright silver tinfoil and sampling products. "Collier's made the greatest fresh fruit ice creams in the summers," Wooden recalled. "You could eat all you wanted, and in those days [I] didn't worry about calories or weight." Sweet treats aside, Wooden's earnings were always modest. Whether employed at the creamery or elsewhere, he recalled it being "tough for a kid to find a job that might earn him a dollar a day."

The return of hoops season in the fall of 1926, on the heels of Wooden's sixteenth birthday, brought welcome, though not surprising, news. Coach Glenn Curtis elevated Wooden to the starting lineup, assigning him to play forward. Senior captain and star player Lester Reynolds and junior Robert Lockhart returned to their guard positions. Rounding out the starting five were sophomore George Eubank at center and freshman Arnold "Sally" Suddith at forward. With preseason expectations running high following the Artesians' runner-up finish in March, players and fans alike eyed a return trip to the Cow Barn in Indianapolis.

Helped by Wooden's speed and blossoming talent on the court, Martinsville won its season opener. The team's record continued to improve, some victories coming by the slimmest of margins, others with embarrassing ease (Artesians 70, Indianapolis Shortridge 11). Steamrolling into the tournament, Martinsville convincingly knocked off nearby schools in sectional competition, and then ruled at the regional games. Even before the regional wins, however, sportswriters buzzed about the team's prospects. "Everybody in is willing to wager a kopek [coin] or two that Curtis and his crew will be in the finals this year," commented a *Kokomo Tribune* writer in late February 1927. "And not a few will lay down several more kopeks that they will stand alone when the racket is over."

On arriving at the Cow Barn in mid-March, the Artesians left little doubt that they wanted to stand alone. In the Friday evening game of the championship series, Wooden and his mates faced Logansport, and the outcome, as a Logansport sportswriter detailed, proved to be decisive: "To those that participated in that fatal game and to the thousands that saw the game, the debacle

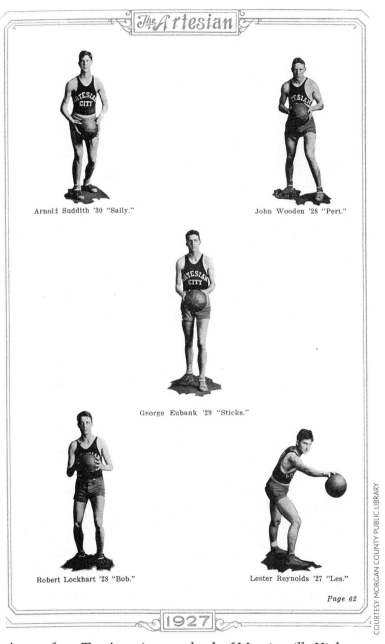

Arnold Suddith '30 "Sally."

John Wooden '28 "Pert."

George Eubank '29 "Sticks."

Robert Lockhart '28 "Bob."

Lester Reynolds '27 "Les."

Page 62

1927

A page from The Artesian *yearbook of Martinsville High School displays the players for the school's 1927 squad, including Wooden, top, right.*

of the court will no doubt long remain a horrible nightmare. Logansport lost and there are no alibis to offer. . . . Martinsville was the best team [27–14]."

Martinsville remained the "best" early Saturday when it beat Gary Emerson, 26–14, followed by an afternoon win over Connersville, 32–21. The evening's title game, officiated by Birch Bayh Sr., forebear of two U.S. senators, pitted the Artesians against the Muncie Central Bearcats. Martinsville had beaten Muncie earlier in the season, but after that defeat the Bearcats had reeled off twenty-three victories in a row. They were anchored by junior Charlie Secrist, a six-foot-five-inch center who years later was inducted into the Indiana Basketball Hall of Fame.

Secrist played well that night, but Wooden's well-balanced performance and team-high ten points helped lift Martinsville to a 26–23 victory and the much sought-after 1927 state title. Wooden's play also earned him All-State recognition and prompted a United Press sportswriter to declare him one of the "finest forwards ever to race up and down the hardwood at a final game." Predictably, thrilled fans immediately mobbed Wooden and his teammates, and the squad received a "tumultuous" late-night welcome upon its return home. In the coming days the celebration continued, as the town honored players with a parade, a banquet, and a community night in the gym, also known as the "Pleasure Resort."

Wooden undoubtedly enjoyed all the fun and festivities. But interestingly, when writing years later about Hoosierdom's "March Madness," he chose to record this: "During my junior year we won the state title by beating Muncie Central, 26–23. I remember that not so much for the victory but for the beautiful silver Hamilton pocket watch that the people of Martinsville gave to each of us on the team. It's a fine watch, and I keep it at home now under a little glass bell. It runs as well as it did on the day I got it."

When school let out for summer vacation, Wooden could not find a job in Martinsville, so he and a friend, Carl Holler, decided to hitchhike west. They hoped to find work harvesting wheat in Kansas and other midwestern states. Though growing numbers of Americans owned automobiles and though all-weather roads were being constructed, hitchhiking in the 1920s was not easy. Outside of Indiana (a leader in paved highway mileage), roads were often gravel, and traffic was light. "There weren't too many cars," said Wooden, recalling how he and Holler stood roadside dressed in their red and blue lettermen's sweaters, a suitcase in one hand and a thumb extended, eyes open for approaching motorists.

They made their way first to Lawrence, Kansas. Having been encouraged by an alumnus, Wooden spoke with famed University of Kansas basketball coach and James Naismith protégé Forrest "Phog" Allen, who invited him to play for the Jayhawks when he graduated from high school. While the boys bided their time in Lawrence, the wheat crop not yet ready for harvest, Allen arranged for them to pour concrete for a new addition to the university's football stadium. After a few days' work to pocket enough cash, Wooden and Holler pushed on, harvesting their way north into the Dakotas. They labored long hours, often fourteen to fifteen a day, but the pay was good. At summer's end, they returned home in time for school and, in Wooden's case, a much-needed reunion with Nellie.

Nellie's parents approved of Wooden. "My mother adored him," Nellie told a writer years later, recalling how John—his head bent down out of shyness—always greeted her parents with a well-

ROBERT LOCKHART "BOB"
Bob has been a regular on the team for
the last three years, playing all positions
on the floor.

JOHN ROBERT WOODEN "JOHN"
Captain John, all state forward, was Mar-
tinsville's star dribbler and basket shot.
His vacancy will be hard to fill.

RECORD OF THE SEASON

November 4, 1927.
The Artesians opened the season this year with a victory over the Washington "Hatchets" on the latter's floor. Final score was 44-25.

November 11, 1927.
The Stone City lads were guests of the Martinsville quintet the following week and two great teams battled to a close game. M. H. S. was victorious, 35-33.

November 24, 1927.
Logansport journeyed south to encounter Martinsville on November 24 and took home the bacon by the tune of 32-23. That third time charm worked.

A write-up in The Artesian *for Wooden's 1928 senior season at Martinsville High School praised him as the basketball team's "star dribbler and basket shot. His vacancy will be hard to fill."*

mannered, "How do?" Nellie's parents were also friendly with Hugh and Roxie Wooden. The two families belonged to the same church (First Christian), attended the same social gatherings, and, as Wooden put it, "visited the same friends." Even better for him, his family had moved in March 1927 to a home on West Washington Street, just five blocks from the Riley home.

While the couple dated in ways typical for the times—they played tennis, went on hayrides, took strolls in the country—their dates on the dance floor were fraught with problems. "I felt like I had two left feet and never could keep time with the music," explained Wooden. Nellie found his awkward footwork perplexing given his nimbleness on the basketball court. Still, the two were often inseparable when basketball was not in season. And in or out of season, they benefited from then-modern technology. "Both of our families had telephones," said Wooden, recalling how their parents surely wondered "how we could talk so long."

Though the high school yearbook listed baseball, track, and math club among Wooden's senior-year activities, he remained fully committed to basketball in the 1927–28 season. Voted captain by his teammates, he worked with Curtis to mold the Artesians into a top-performing squad, and soon victories piled up. Notable that year was a 15–11 win over the Frankfort Hot Dogs, coached by the innovative Everett Case, who later built North Carolina State University into a basketball powerhouse. Notable, too, was an early-season loss to Muncie Central, still chafing from the previous year's defeat in the finals. Muncie beat Martinsville 45–40 in an up-tempo game that did not suit Curtis's style. Both teams itched for a rematch in the tournament. In March, the rematch came.

Having methodically worked their way through the playoffs,
the Artesians and Bearcats met for the 1928 title game in a new
venue—a gleaming, modern facility on Butler University's campus
on Indianapolis's near north side. Capable of seating nearly 15,000
fans, the mammoth basketball arena was the largest in the nation
and destined to become an iconic landmark. It showcased the
Indiana high school tournament finals until 1971 and was the site
of the storied 1954 Milan championship that inspired the popular
movie *Hoosiers*.

The Artesians and Bearcats, however, fixated on more than
scenery at game time. Predictably, the Bearcats were wary of
Wooden, described by one writer as "the tumbling artist from
Martinsville [who] has everything a forward could possibly need.
He is fast, he can dribble like a streak, he can guard, he can shoot

IHS, BASS PHOTO COMPANY COLLECTION, P. 130

*A circa 1946 exterior view of the Butler Fieldhouse on the campus of Butler
University in Indianapolis*

long, and he can twist 'em in as he flies under the basket." The Artesians, in turn, were wary of the Bearcats' superior scoring ability and of their experienced captain, Secrist. A writer who witnessed the game had this to say years later: "The pressure of that night can scarcely be believed. . . . Teenagers like Wooden and Charlie Secrist, Muncie's gangling center, were Hoosier heroes on a par with Babe Ruth and Jack Dempsey."

Confident of Wooden's ball-handling skills, Curtis had devised a strategy that called for a slow, deliberate game. In those days there was no rule that the ball had to be advanced beyond the center line within ten seconds; players could simply stand in the backcourt and hold the ball, as Wooden did that night. When Muncie's defense came after him, Wooden dribbled, passed, or tried a fast break. The stall strategy worked, and Secrist, the tourney's top scorer, was stymied. At halftime, the score was Martinsville 9, Muncie 8.

The pace did not quicken in the second half. With less than a minute remaining and Martinsville leading 12–11, Wooden had the ball and the Artesians seemed to be on their way to another state crown. But then Secrist, who had twisted his ankle earlier in the game, committed what was later described as "the smartest bone-head move in the history of Indiana basketball." Claiming ankle pain, he called a timeout, even though Muncie had used up all its timeouts. The Bearcats were assessed a technical foul and Curtis ordered Wooden to the free-throw line. Wooden argued briefly, thinking it wiser to refuse the free-throw opportunity and instead simply hold the ball until time ran out. But Curtis insisted, and Wooden, who was near perfect the entire weekend in converting free throws, shot and missed. Under the rules at the time, the ball went back to midcourt for a jump ball.

Back in action, Secrist leaped, tipped the ball behind him, and grabbed his own tip, legal in those days. Herb Silverburg, a pioneering basketball writer for the *Muncie Press*, described what happened next:

> One last chance—the timer was clutching his pistol. Still facing away from the Muncie basket, Secrist wheeled and, as he turned, gave one desperate sweep of his arms. Eubank was moving toward the Muncie man with lightning speed. The ball went upward—cleared Eubank's head—continued its flight in a long, sweeping arch—soared onward three quarters the length of the court—started downward. Three thousand Muncie fans on the east end of the big playing floor at the Butler Field House, almost hopeless, watched the career of the ball—hoping against hope. On the west bleachers, Martinsville laughed—it looked like attempting the impossible.
>
> The ball came down—plunged through the cords of the Muncie basket without touching the ring—and Muncie went wild. Martinsville wilted—in the Magic second, men, women and children leaped to their feet frantically—kissing, cheering, slapping each other on the back, tossing hats into the air. And there was 10 seconds to go.

With the ball back at center court, Wooden grabbed the final tipoff, faked a shot, and then passed to teammate Eubank, who put up a shot that spun around the rim. As the ball popped out, Eubank tried to bat it back in. But time ran out, Coach Raymond "Pete" Jolly and the Bearcats clinched their first state championship, and in Muncie, sixty miles from Indianapolis, the partying began. As the Associated Press reported, Bearcat fans joined in the "wildest celebration since the signing of the Armistice."

In the Artesians' locker room afterward, Wooden's teammates sat on benches and, with towels over their head, wept. "That loss . . . is still painful to recall," Wooden wrote decades later. But

THE RUNNERS-UP

The 1927-28 season of basketball has been one of the best in Martinsville High School history. Each year better teams are turned out in Indiana and each year Martinsville teams establish records which will be hard to equal. Although the boys did not win the championship this year, they are at least second best and even this is an honor that few teams have had. With four regulars from last year, an experienced team entered the season's schedule and few teams in Hoosierdom had the honor of downing them. The Artesians were victorious in sixteen of their twenty scheduled games and emerged with high score in eight of their nine tournament games.

John Wooden, Robert Lockhart, Russell Franklin, Marshall Tackett and William Shireman will be lost by graduation, but with two regulars and two substitutes around which to build a team, high hopes of a real team next year are probable.

The boys as they appear in the picture from left to right: Top row: Robert Lockhart, George Eubank, Marshall Tackett, Lloyd Whitlow; second row: Arnold Suddith, John Wooden, Coach Curtis, Russell Franklin, William Shireman; first row: Julius Ellis, Jack Self.

Eighty-two

The Artesian *lauded the 1927–28 basketball team in spite of its defeat in the state championship, noting "they are at least second best and even this is an honor that few teams have had." In the team photo, Wooden is in the second row, second from left.*

disappointed as he was, Wooden did not cry that night. His father's instruction to never whine, complain, or make excuses braced him. So did his father's instruction to always do his best. "I couldn't cry," Wooden said. "The loss hurt me very deeply inside, but I also knew I'd done the best I could do. . . . You lose, you feel bad—sometimes very, very bad. But a much worse feeling is knowing that you haven't done everything you possibly could have done to prepare and compete."

Wooden's performance earned him All-State team honors for the second consecutive year, and Secrist received similar repeat recognition. But for many Hoosiers, then and now, the game's ending is what most merits remembering. With a closing tally of 13–12, the contest was, and still is, the lowest-scoring game in state finals' history. Moreover, Secrist's improbable underhanded heave remains one of the tourney's most famous shots. Wooden certainly never forgot it, and decades later his game memory remained clear: "It seemed to go up through the rafters and came straight down through the hoop."

5

"Goals achieved with little effort are
seldom worthwhile or long lasting."

Purdue University in West Lafayette, Indiana, was in the midst of a building boom when freshman John Wooden arrived in the fall of 1928. Founded as an agriculture and engineering school after the Civil War, Purdue grew steadily during the next half century, and by the 1920s construction workers were either beginning or putting the finishing touches on academic buildings, residence halls, and a 13,500-seat stadium to showcase Purdue's football team. Neither the new buildings nor Boilermaker football drew Wooden to Purdue. Ward "Piggy" Lambert did.

Lambert was Purdue's head basketball coach, a position he had held since 1916, with a year off for military service. According to some accounts, Lambert earned his nickname because as a semiprofessional baseball player he gobbled up or "hogged" balls hit to him at shortstop. By other accounts, the small-framed Lambert "hogged" the ball while playing standout basketball at Wabash College. What was not in dispute was his style of *coaching* basketball. He pioneered the "fast break," which called for players to push the ball up court before the defense had time to set up, enabling quick scores. Wooden had never visited Purdue or even passed through West Lafayette prior to enrolling in 1928. But Lambert's style sold him: "He played the kind of basketball I thought I would like to play."

Other college coaches had courted Wooden in his senior year at Martinsville High School. George Keogan, head coach at the University of Notre Dame in South Bend, had paid Wooden a visit. Coaches at Indiana University, Ball Teachers College (later known as Ball State University) in Muncie, and Butler University had also pitched their programs to him in keeping with the then-standard practice of schools recruiting within a defined geographical area. Wooden had liked Notre Dame's "big name." IU also offered advantages: Wooden could have remained close to Nellie Riley, who had a year of high school to finish. But in the end, he chose Purdue because of Lambert's "fast break" style and because he liked the coach personally: "The way he spoke with my family and with me made it clear . . . he wanted to help make me a man."

With his parents unable to help pay his tuition and with athletic scholarships not what they are today, Wooden had to scramble to finance his education. Lambert arranged for his new recruit to wait tables at the Beta Theta Pi fraternity house, where he became a "brother." Lambert also helped Wooden get a thirty-five-cent-an-hour job in the athletic department, handing out equipment and taping the ankles and arms of athletes in the training room.

Even with those jobs, Wooden looked for other ways to earn a dollar. During football season he sold programs to alumni in hotels and restaurants. He also eventually bought the rights to sell concessions on a special football train that ran between Lafayette and Chicago. In those days, Purdue and the University of Chicago, coached by the legendary Amos Alonzo Stagg, had a fierce football rivalry. On game day, Wooden hired fraternity pals to help him sell sandwiches, candy, and soft drinks to Boilermaker fans aboard the Monon train bound for the Windy City.

Wooden in 1930 as a sophomore at Purdue University.

During the winters, Wooden was equally resourceful. As
an upperclassman, he wrote and published the official Purdue
basketball program, splitting the proceeds with high school
students who sold the dime-a-copy leaflets at home games. He
also persuaded local merchants to donate black and gold ribbon
(Purdue's colors), which he made into lapel pennants and likewise
sold for ten cents. Even the classroom was a place where he saw
financial gain, or at least relief. Under Purdue policy at the time,
students who made the dean's list first semester received free
tuition the second semester, an offer Wooden consistently took
advantage of. "I think I had more jobs in my four years at Purdue
than anyone could possibly imagine," he said, counting his studies
as work.

Wooden had initially planned to study civil engineering,
thinking he someday would like to build bridges and highways.
But engineering students were required to attend weeks-long
surveying camps, not an option for him given his need for
summer employment. In February 1929, early in his second
semester, he transferred out of Purdue's School of Science and
began working toward his bachelor's degree in physical education,
with a new goal to become a teacher and coach. Hoping to teach
English, he loaded up on literature courses, studying the works of

IHS, DC 013

*A panoramic photograph of the Purdue University campus in West Lafayette,
Indiana, circa 1911.*

British and American writers and spending two entire semesters reading the works of William Shakespeare, one semester devoted to *Hamlet*, another to *Macbeth*.

The professor who supervised his readings was M. H. Liddell, a British-educated scholar who wore a bowler hat and high-buttoned shoes and who Wooden characterized as "eccentric." Each semester on the first day of class, Liddell warned students that if they disturbed his trend of thought, they would be ordered to leave and not permitted to return. "And he meant it," Wooden said. "On the other hand, if you made it through the year without interrupting his 'trend of thought,' you'd do fine because he was a great teacher of the classics."

Meanwhile, in the basketball gym, Wooden found himself in the presence of another first-rate teacher—Lambert. Although freshmen were ineligible for varsity action, Wooden scrimmaged hard, determined to build up his stamina and mental toughness. He also worked doggedly to learn Lambert's system of passing, shooting, and moving at a breakneck pace. "Ward Lambert was changing the game—in those days the kind of speed he was putting on the basketball court was almost radical," Wooden said.

Impressed with Wooden's hustle and natural court awareness, Lambert named him a starting guard in his sophomore year, the 1929–30 season. Wooden joined a Purdue lineup that included former Marion High School star Charles "Stretch" Murphy, who had led that team to victory in the 1926 state championship game against Martinsville. Though Murphy was two years older than Wooden, the two struck up a fast friendship, and their talent proved a winning combination for the Boilermakers. Purdue won the 1930 Big Ten championship, and Wooden and Murphy each earned All-American honors. Years later, when recalling Murphy's superb coordination and court skills, Wooden also remembered his tall teammate with gratitude: "I might not have become so well known if I hadn't played with him as a sophomore."

Named team cocaptain for the 1930-31 season, his junior year, Wooden returned to the hardwood with his usual intensity. Standing five-foot-ten-and-a-half-inches tall and weighing 183 pounds, he became a favorite of Purdue fans, who loved watching him dive for loose balls and drive with daring fury toward the basket. He earned such nicknames as the "Human Floorburn" and "India Rubber Man," the latter due to his ability to bounce up off the floor immediately after being knocked down. Fearful his solidly built star guard might land in the stands as he charged forward, Lambert often put Purdue football players at strategic locations as "Wooden" barriers.

Not even the detail-conscious Lambert, however, could control every accident or illness. Wooden spent four consecutive Christmas holidays in the hospital. He came down with scarlet fever in his freshman year, leading to three weeks in a hospital's isolation unit. He suffered a thigh injury his sophomore year when he tried to hop on a truck. As a junior, he gouged out a chunk of flesh when he slipped on a loose plank during practice, an injury that led to an infection. In his senior year, repeated throat infections caused him to have his tonsils removed.

Refusing to let the tonsillectomy slow him down, Wooden, in his final season, led the Boilermakers to a 17–1 record and another Big Ten championship. In an era before postseason collegiate tournaments, the Boilermakers were also named the 1932 national champion team—still the only national

Purdue University basketball coach Ward "Piggy" Lambert (right) had an important influence on the young Wooden (kneeling, center). In 1960 Lambert became a member of the Naismith Memorial Basketball Hall of Fame.

championship in Purdue men's hoops history. Meanwhile, Wooden's personal accomplishments in his senior year included leading the Big Ten in scoring with 154 points, breaking the record set in 1930 (147 points) by Indiana University star and Morgan County chum Branch McCracken. He also was named an All-American for the third consecutive season and the 1932 National Player of the Year. Moreover, his high grade-point average earned him the Big Ten's coveted medal for scholarship and athletic prowess—a medal that Purdue's president, Edward C. Elliott, personally presented him at graduation.

Purdue president Edward C. Elliott holds the Big Ten Medal that he presented to Wooden at the university's 1932 graduation ceremonies. The medal honored Wooden for his combined proficiency in athletics and scholarship.

Although his college playing days were over, Wooden was not
finished with basketball that spring. George Halas, who owned and
coached the Chicago Bears football team and who briefly owned a
basketball team called the Chicago Bruins, hired the Purdue star
to come to the city to play three games. The visit gave Wooden a
chance to demonstrate his skills before new crowds and to earn
$100 a game, the most he had ever made in a lump sum. While
there, a representative from the Rosenblum Celtics invited Wooden
to join that semiprofessional squad and play games around the
country for the then-sizable sum of $5,000 a year. Thinking
the offer "tremendous," Wooden consulted Lambert, and, as he
recounted years later, the conversation went like this:

"What did you come to Purdue for?" [Lambert] asked, after
hearing me out.

"To get an education," I told him.

"Did you get one?"

"I think so."

"You're not going to use it?" he asked.

"I hope to."

"Well, you won't be using it barnstorming around the country
playing basketball. You're not that type of person."

On an earlier occasion, Wooden reported having a similar
conversation with Lambert, this one after scouts for both the
Chicago Cubs and the Cincinnati Reds approached him about
playing minor-league baseball with their organizations. Then, as
would later be the case, Lambert urged Wooden to think about his
future. In both instances, Wooden did, and passed on the offers.

But with his undergraduate education complete, Wooden did
not pass on another offer that spring. At a time when jobs were

scarce due to the Great Depression, he accepted a position to teach, coach, and serve as athletic director at a small high school in Kentucky. He looked forward to heading south, but first he looked forward to seeing Nellie. The two had a date with a preacher.

6

"Failure is not fatal, but failure to change might be."

John Wooden and Nellie Riley picked Monday, August 8, 1932, as their wedding day. Their plans called for a quiet ceremony at the home of an Indianapolis minister because, as Wooden put it, "Nellie's father wasn't well and couldn't afford" a large celebration. The Reverend J. Ambrose Dunkel, pastor of Indianapolis's Tabernacle Presbyterian Church, had officiated at Nell's brother's marriage several years earlier. His services were requested again.

In the months leading up to the wedding, Wooden had been saving money, much of it earned playing basketball around the Midwest. His "life savings" that August totaled $909.05, and two days before the scheduled nuptials he went to his local bank intending to withdraw funds. To his horror, the Martinsville bank had gone out of business, meaning his entire savings were lost. "When the bank went broke, so did I," he said. "I had exactly two dollars to my name, the same two-dollar bill Dad had given me as a graduation gift at Centerton Grade School."

Wooden hurriedly canceled his order for a new car. He and Nell also called off the wedding, leaving them, as Wooden recalled, "totally depressed." But as news of the bank failure spread throughout Martinsville, a local businessman heard about their dilemma and offered to loan the couple two hundred dollars. Though it was not his practice to borrow money, Wooden gratefully accepted the offer, and he and Nell were married as planned, with Wooden's older brother, Maurice, and his wife-to-be, Thelma Williams, driving them to Indianapolis and serving as attendants.

The couple's honeymoon was exceptionally brief, at least according to Wooden's often-told accounts. After spending their wedding night in Indianapolis, he said the couple hurried back to Martinsville early the next morning to meet Coach Ward Lambert, who was driving his former star to a weeklong basketball clinic the coach was running in Vincennes, Indiana. Wooden did in fact work at Lambert's clinic. But his memory apparently failed him as to the time frame. The clinic took place the following week, and, as mentioned in local newspapers at the time, the couple spent their first days of marriage visiting family and taking a trip to nearby Bloomfield, with Wooden also setting aside time to play in an afternoon baseball game at Martinsville. When he eventually headed to Vincennes at week's end, he did so for good reason: "I was going to get $25—a very vital $25 since the loss."

In late August, with the basketball clinic over, the newlyweds moved to Dayton, Kentucky, a factory town near

WOODEN–RILEY

Mr. and Mrs. John Riley announce the marriage of their daughter Nellie to John Robert Wooden, son of Mr. and Mrs. Hugh Wooden, which took place this afternoon in Indianapolis.

The ceremony was performed by the Reverend J. Ambrose Dunkel at his home, 3815 North Delaware street. The bride and groom were accompanied by Miss Thelma Williams and Maurice Wooden, brother of the groom.

The couple started from Indianapolis on a short wedding trip.

Mr. and Mrs. Wooden will leave Martinsville the latter part of August for Dayton, Ky., where they will have a furnished apartment. Mr. Wooden has accepted a position as coach and physical education director in Dayton, a town of about ten thousand, near Cincinnati.

Both are graduates of the local high school, and the groom was graduated from Purdue university in June. Mrs. Wooden is a member of the Tri Kappa sorority and he of the Beta Theta Pi fraternity.

Mr. Wooden's fame as a high school and college athlete has been widespread. Both have many friends.

Wedding announcement for Wooden and Nellie Riley published in the Martinsville Daily Reporter *on August 8, 1932.*

Cincinnati on a bend of the Ohio River. At the time, the Great Depression continued to inflict pain throughout the nation, with millions of Americans unable to find work and with many forced from their bank-foreclosed homes into breadlines. The Woodens owned little themselves—their clothes and a few wedding gifts—when they arrived in Dayton, and they even needed relatives to drive them there. But they felt fortunate on two counts as they set up apartment housekeeping: Wooden had a job and he was to be paid a "fine salary," $1,200 to teach high school English and three hundred dollars to coach the Greendevils.

A photograph of Wooden from the 1934 yearbook, The Pilot, *of Dayton High School in Dayton, Kentucky, where he coached a variety of sports.*

COURTESY DAYTON HIGH SCHOOL

Wooden's latter duty was all-inclusive; he was to coach football, basketball, baseball, and track. The prospect of coaching football worried him, given that Martinsville High School did not field a team when he attended there, and he had little experience playing the game. Hoping to pick up some tips, he consulted that summer with Purdue's coaching staff, but, as he noted, "you don't learn football with talks and diagrams."

During the first week of football practice, one of the lineman decided he had had enough of the new coach's

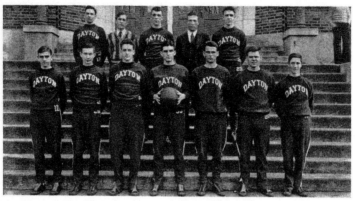

1934 THE PILOT 1934

First Row—Wilson, Stull, Carmichael, Fahrubel, Bertrand, D. Davis, Gray.
Second Row—Beinker, Williams, Mgr., B. Davis, Coach John Wooden, Capt. Smith.

Team photo of Dayton High School's 1934 basketball squad. Wooden is second from right in the back row.

whistle blowing and drills and unwisely mouthed off, right in Wooden's face. Wooden lost his temper, a brief fight ensued, and he ended up feeling ashamed that he had stooped to violence. "It was terrible behavior from someone trying hard to follow the examples of my coaching mentors," he later wrote. "Even more, it went against my father's teaching. . . . These days I'd be fired, rightfully, but on that hot humid afternoon we just moved on and continued practice." That incident aside, Wooden quickly realized he was not qualified to coach football and asked the superintendent to reappoint his predecessor, a request that was granted.

Basketball season brought more headaches for the rookie coach. Wooden tried to teach his players too much too fast and grew irritable when they floundered. "Since everything had come easily for me as a player," he recalled, "I didn't understand why these young men couldn't do the same. It was extremely upsetting to demonstrate something correctly only to watch them do it incorrectly—over and over." During one practice session he became so annoyed with sloppy play that he stormed onto the court and dared the starting lineup to stop him from making a basket. Still muscular and sleek, Wooden darted and dribbled his way through the entire team's defense and scored. Recalling his speed and intensity, one player said later, "If you got near him, you wound up on the floor."

The Greendevils wound up with a roughed-up record—only six victories and eleven defeats that season, with one loss stinging Wooden especially hard. He had arranged for his team to travel to

COURTESY DAYTON HIGH SCHOOL

Dayton High School in Dayton, Kentucky, during Wooden's time there as coach.

Coaches

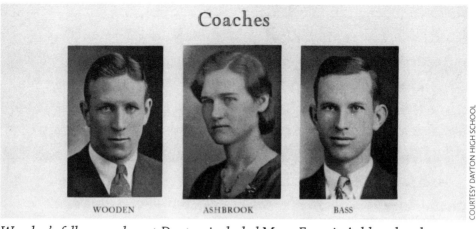

WOODEN   ASHBROOK   BASS

Wooden's fellow coaches at Dayton included Mary Francis Ashbrook, who coached the girls' basketball team, while Willard A. Bass served as athletic director. Bass had also coached both the girls' and boys' basketball teams.

Martinsville in early January 1933 to play against the Artestians, still coached by Glenn Curtis. Wooden knew the competition would be stiff (the Artesians won the state championship later that season, giving Curtis four state titles), and he knew the gymnasium would be packed. But watching his Greendevils lose 27–15 in front of so many of his hometown friends added insult to injury, or, as he later said, it "made the ride back to Dayton seem very long."

For all his struggles as a coach, Wooden judged his first year of classroom teaching a success. He created and followed a detailed lesson plan, figuring out how to cover novels, poetry, and plays in a limited amount of time, using every minute efficiently. He also grasped the need to accommodate students of varying abilities and to appreciate a range of personalities. By year's end, he believed he had learned much about working with and motivating people. Wooden was equally convinced he had learned plenty about himself—"my temper, stubbornness, impatience, and desire for immediate results." When school resumed the following year, he applied his newfound knowledge to the basketball court.

Players responded well to his retooled approach. They sped up play and mastered new techniques, including how to make easy, uncontested shots from the left side of the basket. "We all learned to shoot 'bunnies' with our left hand," recalled reserve forward Ben Stull. When the Greendevils ended the season with a 15–3 record, the school's yearbook proclaimed Wooden's coaching "tip-top" and trumpeted how he "whipped into shape one of the best teams Dayton has sponsored in recent years." Recalled Wooden years later: "I had gone from a goat to a hero in a few short months."

When not coaching, Wooden satisfied his basketball passion by playing weekend games with the Kautskys, a semiprofessional team in Indianapolis named for the club's organizer and owner, grocer Frank Kautsky. Other independent clubs had tried to recruit Wooden, aware that his scoring and tenacious defensive play would draw large crowds. But Kautsky proved the most persuasive, offering to pay the three-time All-American fifty dollars a game plus all expenses—a princely sum in

An All-American basketball player at Indiana University, Branch McCracken coached at Ball State Teachers College before returning to IU in 1938 as its basketball coach. He won two national titles during his twenty-four years at IU.

COURTESY INDIANA BASKETBALL HALL OF FAME

those bleak Great Depression days and more than the twenty-five to forty dollars a game received by Wooden's fellow teammates, among them Emmett "Branch" McCracken and Charles "Stretch" Murphy.

Though money was an attractive feature, semipro basketball had its downside. Hauling his own gear, liniment, bandages, and tape, Wooden had to drive 120 miles from Dayton each week to play Sunday exhibition games in Indianapolis. Then came the return trip: "Sometimes I drove all night, went home, got a shower, put on a clean shirt, and went right to school. . . . I often worked on my

Located at 711 North Pennsylvania Street in Indianapolis and completed in 1926, the Indiana National Guard Armory was later renamed in honor of the person instrumental for its construction, Major General Robert H. Tyndall.

lesson plans as I traveled." Occasionally, he brought along some of his high school players, who watched him in action from behind the bench.

Played on the second floor of the Indiana National Guard Armory in downtown Indianapolis, the games typically pitted the Kautskys against industrial teams from Ohio and elsewhere. Hoosier fans especially liked it when Kautsky arranged matchups with the New York Renaissance, a popular African American squad considered one of the premier teams of the era. "Oh my, those Rens . . . they played a beautiful game of basketball," said Wooden, recalling a 34–28 Kautsky loss to the East Coast club in January 1934. The *Indianapolis News* agreed, telling its next-day readers that the Rens had put on "one of the greatest, if not the greatest, exhibition of basketball ever seen in this city." Against such an impressive team, the *News* added, "even Johnny Wooden's clever dribbling was lost."

Meanwhile, the extra money Wooden earned on weekends came in handy in March 1934 as Nell, at month's end, gave birth to a daughter, Nancy Anne. As if that excitement were not enough, by summer the Woodens were loading their belongings in a van and bundling Nan into the Plymouth sedan. Wooden had accepted an offer to teach and coach at a high school in South Bend, Indiana, a job that promised new challenges, a pay raise to $2,400, and a chance for the new parents to be Hoosiers once again.

7

"Be quick, but don't hurry."

John Wooden might reasonably have had second thoughts about accepting the job in South Bend, Indiana. As he toured the downtown district in June 1934, gunshots rang out. A robbery was under way at the nearby Merchants National Bank, and the outlaws were none other than John Dillinger and his machine-gun-wielding gang.

Known as "Public Enemy Number One," the flamboyant Dillinger terrified the nation briefly during the early 1930s with a series of bank robberies and spectacular jailbreaks. The South Bend robbery was successful; Dillinger escaped that June day with nearly $29,000. But the heist would be his last, as less than a month later he was gunned down by federal agents outside the Biograph Theater in Chicago. Although Wooden and the notorious gangster had no direct acquaintance, they shared common geography. Dillinger spent his teen years in Morgan County and launched his criminal career in Mooresville, not far from where Wooden, seven years younger than the outlaw, grew up.

The jarring welcome aside, Wooden found much to like in South Bend. Situated near the Michigan border, South Bend was bigger and more bustling than either Martinsville or Dayton. A regional industrial hub, it was headquarters in the 1930s to such large manufacturing concerns as the well-known wagon maker turned automaker, Studebaker Corporation. South Bend also sat

Notorious outlaw John Dillinger had little illusions about his career, once noting, "I'm traveling a one-way road, and I'm not fooling myself as to what the end will be."

close to the wooded campus of the University of Notre Dame, where from 1918 to 1930 legendary coach Knute Rockne built the "Fighting Irish" football team into a national powerhouse and popularized the game for ordinary Americans as no coach had ever done before. In Wooden's day, not unlike today, Saturday afternoons in South Bend meant football, and football meant Notre Dame.

Two public high schools served South Bend students in 1934. Wooden joined the faculty at the older, more venerable South Bend Central, located downtown in an imposing brick structure with Gothic-style flourishes. Wooden taught English and at various times coached three sports—basketball, baseball, and tennis. He also served stints as Central's athletic director and managed the business operations of the bookstore, cafeteria, and ticket office.

For all its impressive architecture, Central High, built in 1913, lacked one important feature—a large gymnasium. Basketball practices and home games took place at the nearby Young Men's Christian Association, a workable arrangement though hardly ideal. Central's team, known as the Bears, typically practiced at 6:30 a.m., but players still had to maneuver around a boxing ring, wrestling mats, and gymnastic equipment, not to mention YMCA members who exercised early. The YMCA's dimly lit, unheated locker room, where hot water was always in short supply, presented its own challenges. "Never before or since have I witnessed a team shower and get dressed as fast as those boys did on a subzero morning," Wooden recalled.

In his first year, Wooden assisted Central's head basketball coach, Ralph Parmenter, a fellow Purdue University and Kautsky semipro teammate. The following school year, Wooden became athletic director and, as noted in the yearbook, handed off his

"first mate" basketball duties to another assistant. A year later, Wooden was back with the team, though this time at the helm. After two unimpressive seasons, Parmenter's tenure as head coach was over.

As had been the case in Kentucky, Wooden got off to a wobbly start. The Bears posted an 8–14 record in 1936–37, a losing season overlooked in the Wooden "lore" of later years. (According to the lore, Wooden had winning records throughout his career, except for his first season with the Greendevils.) But lore and lackluster record aside, Wooden

During his thirteen-year career as the football coach at the University of Notre Dame, Knute Rockne led the Fighting Irish to three national titles and had an .881 winning percentage.

COURTESY GREG HUMNICKY

A contemporary photograph of South Bend Central High School.

notched important wins in his first year piloting the Bears. Twice that season Central beat its conference archrival, the Mishawaka Cavemen, a feat the team had not achieved in more than a decade.

Central squeaked by Mishawaka 35–34 in the first battle. The second matchup, on January 29, 1937, promised to be even more of a thriller, and as the *South Bend Tribune* reported the next day, the capacity crowd of 2,000 that packed Mishawaka's gymnasium witnessed "as fiery a skirmish as the teams have ever unfolded in their bitter, ancient rivalry." At halftime, Mishawaka led by six points and later stretched the margin to eight. But Central fought back in the final minutes to gain a 36–32 victory. Then the real fireworks began.

As players headed to the locker room, Wooden and Mishawaka coach Shelby S. Shake met at midcourt where Shake, known for his fiery temper, accused Wooden of "paying" the officials. The dispute escalated, with Shake allegedly using profanity and calling Wooden a name. At that point, according to the *Tribune's* front-page account, "Central's coach quit arguing and started after [Shake]. Members of the crowd which had assembled to hear the dispute got between the rival coaches and prevented bloodshed."

But the theatrics were not over. Fearing that Shake was being mobbed, a Mishawaka player "dove into the pile and put on a flying block that knocked down more persons than any punches swung before or since the dispute had opened." Order was eventually restored, with Shake and Wooden shaking hands and with Mishawaka's principal, Charles Kern, apologizing for Shake's behavior. Shake expressed his own regrets, blaming his outburst on "the heat of the battle." Said Wooden years later about the confrontation: "[Shake] lost his head over losing a close game at home and made some remarks for which he was sorry. He apologized to me that next day and I thought that was the end of it."

Unfortunately for Shake, that was not the end. Arthur L. Trester, the powerful executive secretary of the Indiana High School Athletic Association, began a probe of the incident. It appeared initially that the IHSAA would take no action, preferring to have the two schools resolve the matter. But after the season ended—one in which Wooden's team lost by two points to Mishawaka in the sectional tourney—the IHSAA jolted the state's basketball community by recommending that Shake be relieved of his athletic duties. The IHSAA recommendation was, in fact, an

Shelby S. Shake

order from "Boss" Trester, and that order essentially amounted to Shake being banned from ever coaching again at an Indiana high school. As the *Tribune* bluntly reported: "Arthur Trester's ax fell on Shelby Shake's neck today."

Trester's "ax-falling" sparked strong reaction around Indiana. Even the *Evansville Press*, in the state's far southern corner, objected to the "dictatorial power" Trester wielded in disciplining Shake. Not surprisingly, the *Mishawaka Fair Dealer* declared that Shake had received a "raw deal" and insisted that it was "cock-eyed justice" for Wooden not to be reprimanded as well. Shake, however, declined to protest the ruling and immediately resigned from teaching and coaching, effective at the end of the 1937 school year. He eventually moved out of state and became an assistant professor of industrial education at Southern Illinois University. He died in 1962 without ever again coaching high school basketball.

Decades later, a Mishawaka historian who researched the Shake-Wooden face-off noted that the incident "presents one of the great what-ifs of sports history." Writing in the *Indiana Basketball History Magazine* in 2005, Peter DeKever posed the question of how Wooden's career might have been affected "if the IHSAA had reprimanded or even fired Wooden for trying to punch Shake." DeKever had earlier sought Wooden's thoughts on the matter. In an August 2000 letter, DeKever asked the former South Bend coach for any comments or recollections, and in his usual neat penmanship, Wooden sent a reply that read in part: "Mr. Shake has passed away and it would not help anyone to say anything that would tarnish his name."

Teaching and coaching were not the only activities consuming Wooden's time in the mid-1930s. In July 1936, prior to taking

The Ciesar's All-American basketball team. Wooden is standing, fourth from the right.

charge of the Bears, he became a father again. Nell gave birth to a son, James Hugh. To help pay bills, Wooden edited textbooks for a publishing company and continued to play semipro basketball. The basketball paychecks came from various teams, including one called the Austin Packers in southern Indiana, where Wooden and his brother, Maurice, briefly played together to the delight of downstate Hoosiers. Mostly, however, Wooden took to the hardwood for the Kautskys.

His footwork and speed remained impressive. So did his sharp eye and sure touch at the basketball stripe. In 1935 he thrilled fans at the Indianapolis Armory when he hit his hundredth consecutive free throw, whereupon Frank Kautsky stopped the game and rewarded him with a $100 bill. Wooden later extended that record (over a forty-six-game stretch) to 134 free throws in a row.

Wooden's name retained its star power wherever he traveled
on the semiprofessional circuit. "One time we went to Pittsburgh,"
recalled Kautsky teammate Frank Baird. "That little gym there was
just jammed . . . and the first thing they asked us when we entered
the court there was 'Which one was John Wooden?'" His name
also retained its luster when in 1937–38, having left the Kautskys,
he played briefly for the Ciesar All-Americans, a new Indiana
team based near Chicago. "It was big news when Wooden signed,"
recalled a friend of team sponsor Eddie Ciesar. "I remember the
newspapers making a big splash of it. Attendance at our games
went up, because Johnny was playing."

All the barnstorming, however, eventually made Wooden
road weary. Midway through the 1938–39 season, he rejoined

Wooden, standing, second from left, back row, and the South Bend Central coaching staff relax on the beach at Lake Michigan in 1938. Other coaches are, from left to right: Charlie Stewart, Walt Kindy, Wooden, Chris DalSasso, Bob Primmer, and Bob Jones.

the Kautskys and then, at season's end, called it quits. He was about to turn twenty-nine, his body was showing wear and tear, and his schedule was crammed with family and full-time job responsibilities. Making it easier to put his playing days behind him were the Bears—his basketball team was winning.

In Wooden's second season as head coach, the Bears had reversed fortunes and turned in a respectable 14–6 record. The next season, 1938–39, they went 20–3, and after that they stayed on the victory track. As he had done in Kentucky, Wooden turned his players into high performers by stressing fitness. "He certainly had us in condition. We ran like the wind," said Jim Powers, a Bears forward in the early 1940s. Wooden also remained a hands-on instructor. "He would demonstrate all the time. . . . I swear he ran as fast as anybody on the team, and he could bank a shot from the corner. It was a highlight of practice to see him shoot," recalled Thomas R. Cassady Sr., who while playing on the freshman squad in 1942 observed Wooden in action daily.

A strict disciplinarian, much in the mold of his own coaches, Wooden expected his players to follow training rules that included no smoking, swearing, or violating curfew. He likewise promoted good nutrition and even supplied vitamin pills to players unable to afford them. On road trips, he ordered the team's pregame meal (usually roast beef, toast, lettuce, and vegetables), and players who did not like his selections ate them anyway. "You had to eat the vegetables," recalled former team manager Stan Jacobs.

Wooden's rules aside, players liked how their coach looked out for their interests, whether it be his taping their ankles before practice, helping them with homework after school, or in the case of Ed Ehlers, arranging for surgery on a broken nose.

Ehlers's nose had been cracked a number of times during his three-year varsity career to the point where it became difficult for him to breathe. One day a doctor showed up at the family home and announced he would do the corrective surgery, after which Ehlers went to the hospital, with his cash-strapped family not required to pay a cent. Though never privy to all the details, Ehlers never afterward had any doubts: "I just knew Coach Wooden would take care of it."

Even as he helped players directly, Wooden also influenced them in subtle ways. Years later, many remembered how he was so well read and spoke with such precision. "You'd never hear him using a double negative or end a sentence with a preposition," said Ed Powell, who majored in English in college, a choice he credited to his former coach. Likewise, players also remembered how courteous

The 1940–41 South Bend Central basketball team. Wooden is at the far right, back row, while Ed Ehlers is third from right in the back row, number 35.

and devoted Wooden was to Nell, which they observed firsthand
while riding with the couple to games and eating at their home.

For all Wooden's reserve and gentlemanly ways, however, he
continued to burn with competitive fire. His outbursts, though
rare, were impossible to mistake. During the morning game of
the 1941 semistate competition in Hammond, Wooden went to
the locker room at halftime, unhappy with his team's play against
Lafayette Jefferson. When he discovered the door locked, due to
a tardy janitor, he and an assistant kicked it in and once inside
he "chewed us out like I'd never been chewed out before," recalled
Ehlers, a multisport star athlete. But Wooden's words had an
effect—the Bears won and advanced to the day's second game, one
step away from the state finals.

The day's second contest proved painful, however. The Bears
lost 37–36 to Gary Froebel on a last-second shot, the only time
they trailed. "It was as disappointing a loss as I ever had as a coach,"
Wooden said years later. Ehlers also took the defeat hard: "I never
wanted anything as badly in my life as to win that game."

Nine months later, however, Americans grappled with loss
on a far grander and more sobering scale. On December 7, 1941,
the Japanese attacked the American fleet at Pearl Harbor in
the Hawaiian Islands, killing 2,400 U.S. military personnel and
plunging an ill-prepared nation headlong into war.

"Discipline yourself and others won't have to."

In the months following America's entry into war, John Wooden remained at South Bend Central, coaching the 1941–42 Bears squad to another winning season and then returning to teach and coach again the following school year. In January 1943 he enlisted in the U.S. Navy, a decision that initially did not please Nell. "The only time Nell ever got furious with me was when I enlisted without telling her," Wooden said. Nell, however, had time to get used to the idea. The navy did not call him to active military duty until April.

Drawing on Wooden's experience as a college athlete and a coach, the navy assigned him to be a fitness instructor responsible for getting combat pilots into shape. Commissioned as a lieutenant junior grade, Wooden was sent to various locales, including naval training centers on college campuses. Nell and the two children joined him, an arrangement that allowed the Woodens to maintain some semblance of family life and to take in new sights. In Williamstown, Massachusetts, home to Williams College, daughter Nan recalled how the family lived next to the country estate of a fellow Hoosier, the famous composer and songwriter Cole Porter.

At one point Wooden was to report for duty aboard the USS *Franklin*, an aircraft carrier in the South Pacific. But shortly before his scheduled departure, he underwent surgery for an inflamed appendix and his orders were canceled, after which he remained stateside for the duration of the war. Tragically, the *Franklin* was

The USS Franklin *lists heavily as the result of a Japanese kamikaze attack on March 19, 1945. In spite of severe damage, the aircraft carrier did not sink and managed to make its way to Ulithi atoll for emergency repairs.*

badly damaged in a Japanese dive-bomber attack in March 1945, and among the more than eight hundred crew members who died was the sailor who replaced Wooden, his friend and Purdue University quarterback Fred Stalcup Jr. Reflecting on the incident years later, Wooden wrote: "But for the emergency appendectomy that seemed so unfortunate when it happened, John Wooden's name rather than Freddie Stalcup's would probably have been on the casualty list of dead."

Around Christmas 1945, four months after the war ended, Wooden returned to civilian life. In January he resumed teaching and coaching at South Bend Central, where he steered the Bears to yet another sectional basketball title. Though he was grateful to have his former job back, his military experience had made him restless. Moreover, he was troubled by reports that fellow coaches who had served their country were denied their prewar jobs. "I was treated OK, but I didn't like what I saw happening to friends—other coaches—throughout South Bend," he recalled. In response to what he perceived as "wrong" treatment of his colleagues and to his own stirrings for change, he began looking for work elsewhere.

Wooden had no shortage of job offers, including opportunities to join a book publishing company, work in public relations, and coach at other high schools. But one offer stood atop the others—an invitation from Indiana State Teachers College to coach basketball (and later baseball), teach coaching courses, *and* serve as athletic director, at an annual salary of $3,500. He accepted and in the summer of 1946 moved with his family to Terre Haute.

The decision to uproot was bittersweet. Wooden left behind an enviable record as Central's head coach: 148 wins and 49 losses over the course of eight seasons, for a winning percentage of 75 percent. He also led the Bears to four sectional championships and two regional titles, though much to his regret his record did not include the ever-elusive state crown. Leaving high-school coaching, as he knew full well, meant he would leave that goal unmet. Career issues aside, the move was also difficult for purely personal reasons. Wooden and his family had made many friends in South Bend and had grown to love that northern part of the state. As Wooden told his friend Jim Powers in a letter written decades later: "The older I get the more I reflect about the past and I sincerely believe that the happiest days of my life were the ones spent in South Bend. Had it not been for World War II, I doubt if I would have left Central High School."

* * * *

In 1946 Indiana State Teachers College was what its name stated—a school with a core mission to educate elementary and high school teachers. It was not until the 1960s, a century after its founding and after its mission had expanded, that the school was renamed Indiana State University. The campus occupied the center of Terre Haute, a manufacturing city smaller than, but not unlike, South Bend. The Wabash River ran along the city's western edge, not far from the Illinois border, and Hoosier coal country lay to the south. At the time of Wooden's arrival, the school's enrollment was about 2,300, considerably less than that at the state's two Big Ten schools, Indiana University and Purdue University.

Wooden had been recommended for the head basketball job by his former mentor and high school coach Glenn Curtis. In 1938 Curtis left Martinsville to take charge of Indiana State's basketball squad, and after eight successful seasons as the Sycamores coach, he accepted a job with the Detroit Falcons of the Basketball Association of America. Before leaving for the professional ranks, Curtis urged Indiana State president Ralph Tirey to contact Wooden, which he did. As Wooden noted, Tirey "offered me the job right over the phone."

Wooden did not immediately endear himself to townsfolk. More than 150 basketball hopefuls, many of them returning Sycamore players and Terre Haute athletes, showed up for tryouts that fall, but Wooden passed on most of them. Instead he filled his roster with South Bend-area recruits—young men fresh out of the military whom he knew from Central High or nearby. "I know some of those [Terre Haute] parents and sweethearts and the media were upset by that," Wooden told the *Terre Haute Tribune-Star* years later. "But you have to do what you think is right. You have to rise or you have to fall with it."

The newly assembled squad quickly learned that the new coach meant business. Duane Klueh, a Terre Haute athlete who survived tryouts and became a Sycamore star (and later successfully coached at Indiana State), recalled how Wooden required players to be dressed and in the gym at five minutes past three o'clock each afternoon. If they were a minute tardy, they were not allowed to practice that day. Likewise, players learned—or, in the case of South Bend Central recruits such as Len Rzeszewski, they relearned—that their coach was a stickler for details. "He was the type of guy that taught you to put your socks on, taught you to put your shoes on. He was so strict," said Rzeszewski, recalling Wooden's legendary footwear demonstrations on how to avoid blisters.

The Sycamores opened the 1946–47 season with a loss, fueling more grumbles among fans cool to the new coach. But the team gradually came together and finished with a 17–8 record, including the conference title. The Sycamores also received an invitation to play in the National Association of Intercollegiate Basketball postseason tournament, where they had been runners-up the year before under Curtis.

An aerial-view drawing of Indiana State Teachers College.

Wooden instructs his Indiana State Teachers College team. "Profound responsibilities come with teaching and coaching," Wooden said years later. "You can do so much good or harm."

First staged in 1937 by basketball founder James Naismith, the weeklong event in Kansas City, Missouri, was designed to crown a national champion for small colleges and universities. Though the prestigious tournament offered top-notch competition and provided coaches a chance to burnish their credentials, Wooden declined to attend. A Terre Haute newspaper reported at the time that Indiana State turned down the NAIB invitation for academic reasons—players had already missed too much class time due to road trips. But Wooden later cited an altogether different reason— the NAIB had a policy that forbade African American athletes from participating, and he refused to leave behind Clarence Walker, his team's only black member.

In the 1940s black athletes who played college basketball did so almost exclusively at all-black schools, largely due to discriminatory laws and practices that kept them out of major college programs. When Walker, a freshman from East Chicago, Indiana, showed up for Sycamore tryouts in the fall of 1946, Wooden looked past the young man's skin color, and Walker earned a spot on the team. The East Chicagoan played only a little that season, his role clearly that of a reserve. Still, at tournament time, Wooden stood by Walker. "He was on my traveling squad. I wouldn't take the team and leave him home," he told two Los Angeles sportswriters in the early 1970s for their book *The Wizard of Westwood*. Wooden wrote much the same in his 1972 autobiography *They Call Me Coach*: "They [the NAIB] wouldn't let us bring Clarence Walker. . . . While he didn't play too much compared to our starters, I felt the whole team or no team should go."

Taking a stance against segregation was nothing new to Wooden. He had coached black players at South Bend Central, and when Hoosier restaurant owners sometimes refused service to them on road trips, Wooden had shown his disapproval by exiting with the entire squad, unfed. Before heading to a grocery store to buy bread and lunchmeat, he was known to offer the unwelcoming restaurant owners advice. "I remember him in his polite, beautiful English, telling people that it wasn't going to hurt to have his team eat there with one or two or three black kids eating there," recalled former Bears manager Stan Jacobs, who was Jewish and had experienced discrimination growing up. "He didn't argue, he never got abusive with people, but that stands out for me. It fortified my views on racial equality. . . . John Wooden set [an example] for me of treating people as equal human beings."

Meanwhile, the NAIB tournament went on as scheduled in March 1947, and Wooden, having declined the invitation, let the matter rest. As he wrote years later: "I didn't make any great issue of it, or try to publicize it. I just said 'no.'" But within weeks of Wooden having taken his principled stand, news about another black athlete reverberated throughout the sports world. On April 15, 1947, Jackie Robinson started at first base for the Brooklyn Dodgers, becoming the first African American to integrate major league baseball. The full-blown civil rights movement of the 1960s was still more than a decade away. Nonetheless, the breaking of baseball's color barrier contributed to the social change beginning to sweep across America.

By autumn 1947 signs of more change appeared. The Big Ten, college basketball's most important conference, had previously operated under a "gentleman's agreement" that barred blacks from playing in that league. That September Bill Garrett, a six-foot-two-inch African American center from Shelbyville, Indiana, who had led his team to the state high school championship the previous March, enrolled at IU and joined the basketball program under Coach Branch McCracken. Garrett played on the freshmen team during the 1947–48 season; the next year he became the first African American to be a regular starter on a Big Ten varsity team (Dick Culberson, a reserve on the 1944–45 University of Iowa team, was the first black to play varsity in the Big Ten). A year after Garrett's graduation, six black players suited up for five Big Ten varsity teams, part of a steady march of African Americans into major college basketball programs.

Still, as the 1947–48 season got under way, big-time college basketball remained almost entirely a "white-boys" club.

A November 1948 photograph of Bill Garrett at Indiana University. The Shelbyville gymnasium is named for Garrett, an All-American at IU, who died in 1974.

Moreover, the national postseason tournaments remained *exclusively* white. Walker and Wooden needed no reminder.

9

"If I am through with learning, I am through."

As if coaching, teaching, and serving as athletic director were not enough, John Wooden returned to the role of student while at Indiana State Teachers College. He took classes and wrote a thesis to earn his master of science in education degree. (His thesis, "A Study of the Effect of the Abolition of the Center Jump on the Height of Outstanding College Basketball Players," was completed in August 1947.) In his spare time, he also put final touches on his "Pyramid of Success," a project on which he had worked for years.

The "Pyramid" was inspired in part by Hugh Wooden's advice to all four of his sons: "Don't worry about being better than somebody else, but never cease trying to be the best you can be." Though Wooden heard that advice often while growing up, it was not until he began teaching and coaching in Dayton, Kentucky, that he reflected more seriously on its meaning. Among the questions he pondered were: What really constitutes "success"? Was a sports team "unsuccessful" because it failed to win a championship? Were students "failures" if they received a B or a C grade? Were there other ways to measure success beyond fame, fortune, or power?

By 1934 Wooden had clarified his thinking enough to write his personal definition: "Success is peace of mind which is a direct result of self-satisfaction in knowing you did your best to become the best that you are capable of becoming." Deciding a definition alone was insufficient, he began putting together a diagram in the shape of a pyramid, with fifteen building blocks identifying personal qualities and characteristics that he believed to be essential to reaching one's potential. Among the traits he championed were industriousness, self-control, loyalty, and cooperation.

Throughout the 1930s and early 1940s, Wooden's Pyramid remained a work in progress. He shared it with students, tweaking parts of it as he saw fit, and incorporated it into his coaching classes at Indiana State. By the spring of 1948 Wooden was satisfied that his completed project accurately reflected his philosophy for winning at basketball and life. He also was satisfied that he had designed a useful teaching tool, though he likely never expected the fame that his Pyramid achieved. In the ensuing decades, everyone from coaches to schoolchildren to business leaders asked Wooden for copies, and he dutifully honored the requests by mailing out as many as 1,500 Pyramids a year.

Along with attending to his studies and job at Indiana State, Wooden continued to make time for Nell and their children. Daughter Nan Wooden recalled that her father seldom let his work intrude into family life. "My mother used to say that if she hadn't been at the game, she wouldn't know whether we'd won or lost because that just didn't come home with him," Nan said. The Woodens lived in a rented apartment across from Indiana State's Laboratory School, where Nan and her brother, Jim, along with other faculty children and selected "townies," attended class. The Wooden family's finances at the time ruled out the purchase of a piano and piano lessons, which Nan had long wanted. However, the teacher-training school provided students with free music lessons and take-home instruments on which to practice. "I took up the violin and Jimmy played the big bass fiddle," said Nan, recalling her junior-high years. Any music spilling out of the block-long Laboratory School may have been occasionally muffled, however. The campus gym—home to whistles, cheering, and the thud of balls on hardwood—stood nearby.

Optimism ran high among Sycamore fans at the start of the 1947–48 season, Wooden's second year at the helm, and his team did not disappoint the faithful. Indiana State won eleven of its first twelve games and finished the regular season 23–6, helped by players such as Duane Klueh, Len Rzeszewski, Bobby Royer, Don McDonald, and Jim Powers. Repeating as conference champions, the Sycamores again received an invitation to compete in the

Wooden (back row, left) poses with his 1948 Indiana State team. Clarence Walker kneels near the middle of the first row.

National Association of Intercollegiate Basketball postseason
tournament. But Clarence Walker was still on the squad, and the
NAIB tourney still banned African American players. That being
the case, Wooden, as he repeatedly explained to interviewers in his
later years, had a ready answer. "We were invited again and I refused
because they wouldn't let [Walker play]," Wooden told television
journalist Charlie Rose in 2000. To *Kansas City Star* sports columnist
Joe Posnanski, Wooden said as much in 2002: "I refused to go to the
[1948] tournament if Clarence couldn't go."

Given Wooden's progressive views on race, he may have *tried* to
turn down the NAIB bid. But newspaper accounts from that era tell a
different story. On February 22, 1948, with the NAIB racial ban still
in effect, the *Terre Haute Sunday Tribune* reported that Indiana State
would play in the tournament. "Wooden revealed that his squad will
be in Kansas City for the national on March 6," sports columnist Bob
Nesbit told readers. Three days later, on February 25, the *Tribune*
again reported that the Sycamores would soon "play in the National
Collegiate Tourney in Kansas City." And on February 29, under the
headline "Indiana State Will Invade Kansas City," the *Sunday Tribune*
published what by then was official: "John R. Wooden . . . has
announced that his Sycamores have accepted" the NAIB invitation.
The newspaper listed twelve players who were certified to represent
the team. Walker's name was not included.

Walker kept a diary during the 1947–48 season, and his account
supports what the *Tribune* reported—namely, that he was not slated
to make the trip. Walker first sensed something was afoot when he
saw his teammates signing a paper—the tournament entry form—
in the locker room in late February before a game with Valparaiso
University. Walker was not asked to sign, leading him to broach the

Walker during his playing days at Indiana State.

subject with his coach. "When I first came to the game my mental attitude was tops," he wrote in his diary. "I was happy, etc. In fact I think I was too happy and [it] seems that whenever I am too happy, something happens to me for the worse. It did. I asked Wooden what the dope is on the Kansas City tournament. In his suave but candid way he told me . . . that Negroes could not play."

As a young black man, Walker was no stranger to bigotry, and it was precisely because of a "color barrier"—not just in college sports but in all aspects of American society—that he was moved to keep a diary his sophomore season. He titled his journal "Mr. J.C." for

The Municipal Auditorium in Kansas City, Missouri, hosted the first National Collegiate Basketball Tournament in 1937. The facility has long hosted tournaments, including in 1948, when Wooden took his Indiana State team there.

the so-called "Jim Crow" segregation laws and racist traditions in place at the time, and he recorded his thoughts "as a way of getting something off my mind." His journal recounted numerous examples of racial slights and discrimination that he endured throughout the season—from a waiter failing to take his order as the team sat at a drugstore counter in South Bend to his having to stay apart from his squad in a "Negro hotel" in Jeffersonville, Indiana, when the team played Eastern Kentucky University. "I probably could not have been able to play had the game been played in Kentucky," he wrote.

Walker also recorded incidents of ugly name calling. During a game in Terre Haute, according to his journal, he heard the opposing coach holler "Jerk that nigger's head off" as Walker battled for a rebound against a player from Southeastern (Oklahoma) State College. The yell did not go unnoticed. "Mr. Wooden heard him and told him, 'Why don't you go back to Oklahoma.' After the game, Mr. Wooden went into their dressing room and there was a big argument," Walker wrote.

While pouring out his frustrations and expressing his hurts, Walker also made clear on the journal's opening page that he highly regarded his coach: "My opinion of Johnny Wooden, the coach of our basketball team, is that he is a wonderful coach. He is brilliant in knowledge of basketball. As far as I know, he is not bias [sic]. . . . If all people were in mind as he is in character, I think Mr. J.C. would be trivial." Walker also defended Wooden against another charge. "Someone rumored that Wooden favored the South Bend boys," Walker wrote. "Frankly, I say he did not favor the South Bend boys. Everyone got what he deserved. 'If you looked good, you played.'"

Walker admitted to being stung when Wooden told him he would not be going to Kansas City. "Believe me," Walker recorded, "it is hard to take." Moreover, because of "Jim Crow" laws throughout the South and in parts of the Midwest, Walker also understood that he would not play in the last two regular season games on February 27 and 28 in Saint Louis and in Jonesboro, Arkansas. "Another one of those understandable deals," he wrote. "Officially, my season is over Tuesday the [February] 24th when we play Illinois Normal at home."

Walker's season did not end early, however. Just three days before the NAIB tournament began on March 8, the organization's executive committee rescinded the ban against black players. The abrupt about-face came not because of pressure from Wooden or Indiana State, which had already made clear the Sycamores would compete. Rather, NAIB officials took action because of fast-breaking developments that threatened to weaken competition and undercut the tournament's prestige. Specifically, during the first week of March three Eastern colleges—Manhattan College, Siena College, and Long Island University—turned down invitations to play in the thirty-two-team single-elimination tournament because of the rule barring blacks. The U.S. Olympic Committee also indicated it might exclude the tourney winner from participating in the upcoming Olympic trials unless the ban was lifted. As the Associated Press reported at the time: "The National Intercollegiate Basketball tournament opened its door to Negro players Friday [March 5] to make sure of representation in the playoffs for an Olympic berth. The executive committee of the Association, facing the Olympic situation as well as rejection of bids by several teams, voted in a telegraphic poll to rescind the tournament racial ban."

With the Sycamores set to leave Terre Haute on Saturday, March 6, Wooden reached out to Walker. "Mr. Wooden readily understanding the situation got in contact with me and talked the deal over," Walker wrote in his journal. The National Association for the Advancement of Colored People, an organization at the forefront of promoting equal rights for blacks, weighed in on the rule change and, according to Wooden, urged Walker to go. By Saturday, the *Tribune* brought readers up to date: "Yesterday in Kansas City tourney officials made a ruling that Negro players would be eligible to compete. . . . This will permit Clarence Walker, speedy State guard, to play and Coach Wooden immediately placed him on the squad."

Coach Wooden and Walker during the 1947–48 season. At the end of his journal, Walker noted of Wooden, "If all people were in mind as he is in character, I think Mr. J.C. [Jim Crow] would be trivial."

Pleased as he was to go, Walker suffered indignities throughout the trip. When the Sycamores stopped for lunch that Saturday, the restaurant refused to serve him, prompting Wooden to walk out with the entire team. When the Sycamores stopped that night in Columbia, Missouri, the hotel manager refused to allow Walker to room with his teammates. Instead, he was given a cot in the basement, next to a foul-smelling bathroom frequented by loud and boisterous college students partying into the early morning hours. "One can guess how much sleep I got," Walker wrote. On the return trip home, Walker did not fare much better. When the team stopped for the night in Effingham, Illinois, he again had to sleep in a hotel basement, segregated from the other players.

Walker, however, made history that March. When Wooden sent him onto the court in the Sycamores' NAIB opener in Municipal Auditorium in Kansas City, he became the first African American to compete in a national college basketball tournament. Walker scored three points as the Sycamores trounced Saint Francis University (Pennsylvania) by a 72-40 score. Indiana State continued winning, knocking off three more teams and earning a berth in the championship game at week's end against the University of Louisville. The Sycamores battled hard, but ultimately lost 82–70. Their 27–7 season record would not be surpassed until the 1978–79 season, when a Sycamore team captained by the legendary Larry Bird went 33–1.

In spite of breaking a racial barrier, Walker, who scored a total of eight points that week, did not receive much attention in the press. The day after his trailblazing appearance, the *Kansas City Star* made no mention of it being a tournament first. Likewise, white-owned newspapers in Indianapolis and Terre Haute let the moment pass without comment. Kansas City's black newspaper, *The Call*, took note of Walker's pioneering role by reporting that "no expressions of disapproval were heard" from spectators and opponents regarded him "as just another basketball player."

But with or without press coverage, Walker and Wooden helped put college basketball on a path from which there was

COURTESY INDIANA STATE UNIVERSITY ARCHIVES

Wooden addresses his Indiana State team in the locker room. One of Wooden's many sayings to his players was, "Be quick, but don't hurry."

no turning back. The following year, in 1949, three teams with black players competed in the NAIB tournament. In 1950 a team with two black starters competed in both the National Invitation Tournament and the National Collegiate Athletic Association tournament, thus integrating those two high-profile contests. And in 1953 the NAIB (renamed the National Association of Intercollegiate Athletics, NAIA) became the first collegiate organization to open its membership to historically black colleges. That set the stage for 1957 when Tennessee A & I State University became the first historically black school to win a national basketball title.

In later decades, Wooden appeared at ease talking about Walker and the civil rights milestone achieved in 1948. Missing from Wooden's public remarks, however, was any explanation as to why Indiana State accepted the tournament bid *before* the racial ban was rescinded. Wooden also never publicly explained why his later comments about "refusing" the NAIB's invitation contradicted what the *Tribune* reported in 1948 and what Walker's diary recorded. In a 2014 biography titled *Wooden: A Coach's Life*, author Seth Davis offered one explanation for the discrepancy. "Like many compelling storytellers, especially the ones who tell stories about themselves, Wooden sometimes had trouble separating fact from fiction," Davis wrote. He also argued that Wooden engaged in "revisionist history" and "exaggerated his role in desegregating the tournament."

The fairness of that assessment remains open to debate. Among the unknowns is how much pressure, if any, Indiana State administrators put on Wooden in February 1948 to set aside his personal disdain for bigotry and accept the NAIB's invitation. Kevin Jenison, media relations coordinator for Indiana State University's athletic department, said it is his understanding—based on information passed down through campus channels over the years—that the university believed its "interests would be better served" if the team competed in Kansas City. "It was out of John's hands. The university had the final say," Jenison said.

Jenison added that Indiana State, having declined the bid the previous year, knew that NAIB officials were wrestling over whether to rescind the racial ban. "The University knew there was this push to get the rule changed . . . so they decided to accept the bid and see what happened," said Jenison, noting that school officials may also have been motivated by practical considerations given that "it's not easy to change itineraries and schedules." In short, according to Jenison, the university "hoped" that behind-the-scenes pressure prior to the tournament would result in "everything getting worked out . . . and it eventually did."

As for Walker, the year 1948 was not the last time he played basketball in Kansas City. He was a Sycamore senior starter in 1950 when Indiana State won the NAIB championship under another coach, Wooden by then having moved on. After college, Walker had a successful career as a teacher, counselor, and assistant school superintendent in East Chicago and taught tennis for more than thirty years in Indiana and Illinois. He died in 1989.

In Walker's last dated journal entry following the 1948 basketball season, he took note of the news that Wooden had accepted a new job. "A week ago it was publicly announced that John R. Wooden . . . will not return next year," Walker wrote on April 26. His next comment was succinct: "A truly wonderful man is leaving."

10

"The only place that success is before work is in the dictionary."

In the summer of 1948, John and Nell Wooden loaded their two children into their car for a trip across the continent on Route 66. After two leisurely weeks, with stops at Carlsbad Caverns, the Grand Canyon, and other sightseeing attractions, the family arrived in Southern California to sweet-smelling orange groves and sun-dappled palm trees. In Los Angeles, their destination, they encountered something less inviting. "We got on the Pasadena Freeway and it almost scared us to death," said Nell, recalling their first venture onto a parkway famous for its tight curves, narrow lanes, and busy traffic. "I remember John getting all upset and saying to us, 'What are we doing here, anyway?'"

They were "here" for Wooden's new job: head basketball coach at the University of California, Los Angeles. He had accepted the position in April, a month after Indiana State Teachers College's impressive showing at the National Association of Intercollegiate Basketball tournament and after compiling a 44–15 record in his two years with the Sycamores. Bob Kelley, who broadcasted football and basketball games in Indiana and who eventually became the radio voice of the Los Angeles Rams, had recommended Wooden to UCLA officials. Emmett "Branch" McCracken, who turned down the UCLA job in 1947 and 1948 to remain head coach at Indiana University, also had passed along Wooden's name.

Other colleges had courted Wooden that spring, among them the University of Minnesota, a Big Ten Conference school with a huge field house. Wooden had planned to accept Minnesota's offer, largely because he was eager to coach in the Big Ten and because relocating there meant he could remain in the Midwest. But before committing to the Golden Gophers, Wooden had sought assurances he could choose his own staff—a matter that Minnesota athletic director Frank McCormick had to submit to an athletic board. McCormick had promised to telephone Wooden at 6:00 p.m. on Saturday, April 17, with a decision. Meanwhile, Wooden had arranged for UCLA's athletic director, Wilbur Johns, to call

Wooden and his wife, Nell, at their home in Terre Haute, Indiana, shortly after he accepted the head coaching job at the University of California, Los Angeles, in 1948.

at 7:00 p.m., at which time he assumed he would politely decline the Bruins offer. Minnesota officials approved Wooden's request, and McCormick dutifully tried to call Wooden at 6:00 p.m. But a freak snowstorm temporarily knocked out telephone service in the Minneapolis-Saint Paul area. As Wooden waited at home, unaware of the problem, his phone rang promptly at 7:00 p.m. with Johns on the line. Having heard nothing from Minnesota, Wooden accepted the West Coast offer. When McCormick called later that night, phone service restored, he wanted Wooden to call Johns back and wriggle out of the deal. But Wooden refused: "I had accepted."

In 1948 UCLA was a young institution, its reputation as a top-tier academic and athletic school still in the making. The school had opened in 1919 as a branch campus of the University of California, headquartered four hundred miles north in Berkeley overlooking San Francisco Bay. The "Southern Branch," as the downtown Los Angeles campus was then known, was renamed UCLA in 1927. Two years later the school moved from downtown to a spacious new campus in west Los Angeles, once the site of bean and barley farmlands at the base of the Santa Monica Mountains. The campus adjoined a village called Westwood, and it sat close to Beverly Hills and Bel Air, then and now home to the rich and famous. Five miles away, down Sunset Boulevard, lay the Pacific Ocean.

As was the case at colleges across the nation, UCLA's enrollment swelled after World War II, climbing from roughly 7,000 students in 1937 to 13,800 in 1946. Returning veterans enrolled in classes; so did transplants from other parts of the country, lured to California by its surging economy and comfortable weather. The influx of students did not alter one fact, however: UCLA remained largely a commuter campus, and in such an environment, athletic traditions

were slow to develop. Moreover, commuting UCLA students did
not really need a campus to enjoy sports or pursue fitness. They had
an ocean to surf in and mountains to climb, and if beaches were
too crowded for volleyball, the tennis courts and golf courses were
always open for play.

The season before Wooden's arrival, the UCLA basketball team
had posted an overall record of 12–13 and tied for last place in the
Pacific Coast Conference. Fans were not surprised. Since joining the
PCC in 1928, the Bruins had had only four winning seasons and few
standout athletes. Among the most noteworthy players were Ralph
Bunche, a star in the 1920s who later achieved fame as a Nobel
Peace Prize winner; Major League Baseball pioneer Jackie Robinson,
who lettered in four sports while at UCLA from 1939 to 1941; and
Don Barksdale, who was the first African American to be named an
National Collegiate Athletic Association All-American (1947) and
the first to make an Olympic basketball team (1948).

With or without a new coach, sportswriters did not foresee a
quick turnaround in the Bruin program. They predicted UCLA would
finish last in the conference in the 1948–49 season, and Wooden
initially was hard-pressed to disagree. Upon accepting UCLA's offer,
he had taken a brief leave from Terre Haute to meet Bruin players
and put them through a week of spring practice. What he saw then,
and again in the fall, left him dismayed: "I sure didn't see many
basketball players among that new bunch. Boy, it looked pitiful, a
motley crew like I had in physical education classes back at Indiana
State." The spring practice had been especially disheartening: "I was
shattered. Had I known how to abort the agreement [with UCLA] in
an honorable manner, I would have done so and gone to Minnesota,
or if that was impossible, stayed on at Indiana State."

Just as the lack of talent made Wooden wince, so did the facilities. The Bruins practiced and played on the second floor of the Men's Gymnasium, nicknamed the "B.O. Barn" because of the foul smell caused by poor ventilation. The Romanesque-style brick building could hold 2,400 fans on pullout bleachers, a fraction of the seating capacity in many Hoosier gyms, including the one in Martinsville. But lack of seating seldom caused headaches. At the time of Wooden's arrival, sellout crowds were rare. Bad odors and limited seating aside, the gym was also not, in Wooden's words, "conducive to good teaching." Gymnasts and wrestlers worked out each afternoon when the team did, adding to the noise and cramped conditions and making private meetings impossible. Making matters worse, the dingy facility had only two baskets, and dust fell liberally from the rafters.

When he interviewed for the job, Wooden had been told the gym would be replaced with a modern one within three years. Until then, he resolved to make the best of a poor situation, and in what became a ritual, he and Ed Powell—who had played for him at South Bend Central High School, assisted him at Indiana State, and followed him to UCLA—started the coaching portion of each day as janitors. They filled two buckets with hot water and mopped the floor, ridding it of dust, gymnasts' chalk, and other debris before the start of 3:30 p.m. practice.

As he had done for years, Wooden taught a fast-break, end-line-to-end-line pressure style of play. West Coast teams were not wholly familiar with that type of running game, but UCLA players—tired of the slowdown, walk-the-ball-up-the-court approach—liked it. The team included a returning Bruin who Wooden met for the first time that fall: six-foot-three-inch guard

George Stanich, who had been busy pitching baseball for UCLA
in the spring and winning a bronze medal in the high jump at the
summer Olympic Games in London.

To nearly everyone's surprise, the team got off to a strong start.
In mid-December 1948 a writer for the *Eugene (OR) Register-Guard*
declared that Wooden had already "brought the Bruins up from

Throughout his career, Wooden took and kept meticulous notes.

nowhere to become the coast's first and foremost 'dark horse' of the 1949 season." The writer also noted what was becoming obvious: "The Bruins . . . run like a bunch of thieves and hang onto the ball like they own it."

UCLA continued blitzing its way to victory and ended up with twenty-two wins—the most in the school's history. It finished first in the Southern Division of the PCC, with the Bruins then competing in a best-of-three series for the conference title. The team ultimately lost that series to the Northern Division's Oregon State University. But as Wooden later wrote, the season was "perhaps the most satisfying year of my entire teaching and coaching career." The *Daily Bruin*, UCLA's yearbook, described the season this way: "Taking over only an average group of boys, Jovial John proceeded to bamboozle the world of sports by producing the scrappiest aggregation of lanky lems ever to set foot on a Bruins hardboard-patch."

The next year the well-conditioned Bruins, still scrappy, still hustling, repeated their winning ways. The team chalked up twenty-four victories and captured the conference crown, sending UCLA to the NCAA tournament for the first time in school history. The Bruins matched up well in the first round of the regional playoffs against Bradley University and appeared poised to win. But in the final minutes the Bruins fell apart, losing 73–59 and leading Wooden to say later: "It was just a classic example of how to lose a basketball game you had won. I had not properly prepared my players and had no one to blame but myself."

Despite the disappointing loss, UCLA fans reveled in the team's upward trajectory. At the same time, Wooden's coaching accomplishments caught the attention of other schools, among them his beloved alma mater, Purdue University. The Boilermakers had just ended the 1949–50 season tied for eighth in the Big Ten, and ever since Ward "Piggy" Lambert's retirement several years earlier, Purdue's basketball program had languished. Hoping to jump-start it, Purdue made Wooden an offer that was, in his words, "almost unimaginable." He was to receive a salary higher than the $6,000 he earned annually at UCLA, a new car every year, a country club membership, a home on campus, and other enticing benefits. The offer meant his dream of coaching in the Big Ten could be fulfilled. But first he had to settle up with UCLA.

At issue was his three-year contract. In a meeting with UCLA officials, Wooden politely asked to be released from the third and final year of the contract, a request not well received. Those officials reminded Wooden that he had insisted on a three-year deal and they expected him to honor it. "They made me feel like a heel for even considering leaving," Wooden recalled.

Irritated, but also a man of his word, Wooden agreed to stay at UCLA for one more year. He held out hope that the Boilermakers would ask him again the following season, and he promised Nell they would then return "home where we belonged." Meanwhile, Purdue hired one of Wooden's former college teammates, Ray Eddy, as head coach for the 1950–51 season. Two years younger than Wooden, Eddy had ample reason to celebrate in the summer of 1950. He had just landed a big-time college job, and, equally important, he had just coached Madison High School to the Indiana state basketball championship—the very championship Wooden would have liked for his résumé.

11

*"Things turn out best for the people who make the
best of the way things turn out."*

John Wooden's disappointment at having to pass on Purdue
University's offer was coupled that summer with sorrow. His father,
Hugh, died on July 3, 1950, at the age of sixty-eight following
an illness. Notified of Hugh's weakening condition, Wooden had
returned to Martinsville, Indiana, and was present at the time of
death. Hugh was buried in Centerton Cemetery, alongside his two
daughters and not far from the farm where the family had long
resided. Writing later about his father's passing, Wooden said: "The
man who had given me the compass I followed in life was gone."

Back in Los Angeles, Wooden and Nell worked at shaking
off bouts of homesickness. They missed the Midwest's changing
seasons and disliked how, as Wooden said, "Christmas felt like
summer." Likewise, Los Angeles's freeways still scared them, and
they often felt out of place at West Coast social gatherings. In
Indiana the couple had friends who drank and served alcohol, but
Wooden insisted that those friends never criticized him or Nell for
abstaining. In Los Angeles, he felt different: "I was a teetotaler who
. . . was made to feel uncomfortable about it."

The Woodens lived in Mar Vista, a growing community on Los
Angeles's west side and a short commute from campus. Soon after
arriving in California, Wooden had cashed in his retirement plan

at Indiana State Teachers College for a down payment on the new
home. He had also taken a summer job—one he returned to for
several summers—to make the mortgage payments. Working as an
early-morning dispatcher for a dairy in Venice, California, he issued
orders to delivery drivers and then after finishing paperwork and
sweeping the dairy office, he headed to his "day" job at UCLA.

While money was not plentiful in the Wooden household,
neither was it wasted. Wooden had been raised to live modestly,
and he knew how to stretch a dollar. His daughter, Nan, recalled
a time in South Bend when her father squeezed oranges into a
pitcher, only to accidentally knock the pitcher over. "He mopped the

© BETTMANN/CORBIS

*An early 1950s photo of Wooden with Ed Powell (left), his varsity assistant,
and Alan Sawyer (right), junior varsity coach. A Hoosier native, Powell played
for Wooden at South Bend Central High School, was assistant coach at Indiana
State Teachers College, and followed him to UCLA in 1948. Sawyer was a
starting forward on Wooden's first two UCLA teams.*

floor with a towel and squeezed the juice back into the pitcher," she said. "He said it was no problem because mom was a meticulous house cleaner."

As they had done in Indiana, Wooden and Nell continued to make family time a priority. Sunday was explicitly set aside for family activities, with the day typically beginning at church. The Woodens attended the First Christian Church in Santa Monica, where, on the first Sunday that they worshipped there, Wooden was surprised to learn that the pastor was Reverend Wales E. Smith, a high school classmate of his. "I had known a Wales Smith . . . but as far as I knew, he was a pastor in Kokomo, Indiana," said Wooden, recalling his pleasure at reconnecting with someone from Martinsville. A lifelong churchgoer, Wooden eventually served as a deacon at First Christian.

Wooden's attachment to Nell and the children had a direct bearing on one aspect of his job: recruiting. Rather than search far and wide for players, requiring trips away from home, he looked for talent primarily in Southern California, and he especially zeroed in on players at the many community colleges around Los Angeles. West Coast high school players, in his opinion, were not as well schooled in basketball fundamentals as Indiana's prep athletes. Wooden expected that skill disparity to disappear over time as the sport caught on among California youth. But until then, he concentrated on recruiting athletes with junior college experience and, as much as possible, he scouted locally: "I made that clear when I came [to UCLA]. . . . I would not be away from home," said Wooden.

Determined to finish out his contract with his winning record intact, Wooden steered the Bruins to their third straight division title in 1951. At season's end, following a loss in the conference playoffs, he considered his options for moving elsewhere, and they turned out to be few. Purdue did not make him an offer that spring. Neither did anyone else. By then, his teenage children had made new friends and Nell, pleased that the children were happy, was pursuing her own interests, among them golf. That left Wooden to confront the undisputed facts—he was forty years old, had been coaching for nearly two decades, and had yet to win a major championship. At UCLA his teams were winning and fans were supportive. Staying, he concluded, made good sense.

Beyond those considerations, Wooden was aware that Los Angeles's population was growing rapidly, meaning that the pool of area basketball talent was certain to increase. In addition, he enjoyed working with athletic director Wilbur Johns, and he respected UCLA as an academic institution. To the relief of Johns, varsity club boosters, and other university officials, Wooden renewed his contract and mentally crossed a threshold: "California was going to be our permanent home."

As he shifted his thinking to building UCLA's basketball program over the long term, Wooden had to contend with another program— football. The year after his arrival, UCLA hired Henry "Red" Sanders as its new football coach. Hard driving and witty, Sanders wasted no time making his presence felt on campus, both in terms of lobbying for additional funding and building the football team into a national power. Between 1949 and 1958, when Sanders died suddenly of a heart attack, he led the single-wing Bruins to three conference titles, two Rose Bowls, and a shared national championship in 1954.

The money and media attention directed at UCLA football led to some tension between Wooden and Sanders. Observed sports columnist Melvin Durslag of the *Los Angeles Herald-Examiner*: "Some strong feelings developed . . . but John suffered in silence and never made a public issue of his grievance." By 1955, however, UCLA football was the least of Wooden's worries. Still without a new basketball arena, the university received word from fire officials that crowd size had to be limited in the old basketball gym. Due to safety concerns, no more than 1,300 people would be allowed to attend games.

Rather than limit attendance, and lose needed athletic revenue, UCLA officials scouted around for off-campus gyms. That first season the Bruins hosted opponents in places ranging from the Venice High School gym to the Pan-Pacific Auditorium in downtown Los Angeles. The Pan-Pacific served as home base for the next three seasons, with other gyms thrown into the mix. Starting in 1959 the Bruins played in the new Los Angeles Memorial Sports Arena, sharing that blue-domed modern venue with their downtown arch-rival, the University of Southern California Trojans.

For UCLA's opponents, the school's decision to abandon the "B.O. Barn" came none too soon. Visiting coaches dreaded playing in the "sweatbox," and they even accused Wooden of cranking up the heat inside so as to make opposing players tire more easily. Wooden denied any thermostat tampering; his Bruins survived the hot conditions, he explained, because they were superbly conditioned. But temperatures aside, visiting teams disliked the gym because UCLA fans, their numbers increasing since Wooden's arrival, sat close to the court action, their ear-deafening hoots and hollers intended to agitate opponents. Writing in early 1955 a San Francisco area sportswriter called UCLA fans "as hostile a crowd as there is in college basketball today."

UCLA players John Moore (left, under the basket) and Eddie White try to stop Niagara University's Ed Fleming from passing the ball during the Eastern College Athletic Conference Holiday Festival at Madison Square Garden, December 27, 1954.

Meanwhile, the Bruins continued to practice in the "B.O. Barn," with Wooden and his assistants continuing their floor-mopping ritual. When the Los Angeles Sports Arena opened, UCLA occasionally scheduled practices there, but negotiating the fourteen miles of traffic to get downtown was, as Wooden said, "a hassle." The Sports Arena was less than ideal on game day as well. The arena sat close to the USC campus, making it convenient for Trojan fans to stop by to root against the Bruins.

Gym headaches aside, UCLA won the 1951–52 conference championship. The Bruins again advanced to the NCAA Regionals, though, as was the case two years earlier, they stumbled in the tournament's first round. During the next three years Wooden kept the wins coming by coaxing good performances from his players, most of them of middling ability, others a notch above. For scoring help during that period, he looked to six-foot-five-inch forward John Moore, a Gary, Indiana, native who started all four years and who was one of only a few Hoosiers Wooden ever coached at UCLA.

An African American, Moore arrived at a time when blacks were expected to live elsewhere in Los Angeles, not in whites-only Westwood. Moore initially found housing in a black neighborhood, but he soon became frustrated about having to travel so far to campus. Sensitive to Moore's predicament, Wooden enlisted the help of UCLA's recently graduated student body president, an African American named Sherrill Luke. Well acquainted with Wooden, Luke arranged for Moore to live in a nearby Jewish fraternity, where Luke had resided and still had friends. Meanwhile, Moore's girlfriend and eventual wife, Algene, appreciated the courtesy that Wooden and Nell regularly extended to her. "They always acknowledged and made me feel good at home there in the basketball gym," recalled Algene, who was married to the UCLA Hall of Famer for thirty-two years before his death in 1987. "Color didn't matter to the Woodens. My husband just loved him."

In 1955–56, the year after Moore's graduation, the Bruins went undefeated in their conference and advanced for the third time to the NCAA tournament. Still, not even the considerable talent of Bruin center and eventual National Basketball Association All-Star Willie Naulls could help UCLA reverse its pattern. The Bruins fell, yet again, in the first round of the regionals. Their opponent was the University of San Francisco, the defending national champion in the midst of a sixty-game winning streak. USF was powered by six-foot-nine-inch center Bill Russell, whose shot-blocking and rebounding skills eventually propelled USF to its second consecutive national title. Within months, Russell went on to win a gold medal as captain of the U.S. basketball team in the 1956 Summer Olympics. He then joined the Boston Celtics, quickly becoming a superstar and remembered today as one of the NBA's best players.

Russell and the USF Dons did not leave UCLA completely demoralized in the 1956 playoffs, however. The next night the Bruins beat Seattle University in the consolation game, giving Wooden his first NCAA Tournament win. Still, a consolation game win in three NCAA appearances was adding up to tournament troubles for Wooden. His Bruins were underperforming at season's end, something that he admitted "disturbed" him. His friend Emmett "Branch" McCracken had already led Indiana University to two national titles, one in 1940 and another in 1953. The University of Kentucky's Adolph Rupp had recently clinched three titles for the Wildcats—in 1948, 1949, and 1951. And now a team up the coast, USF, had won back-to-back titles. As he approached age forty-six, Wooden still had no "big" win attached to his name, and more headaches loomed—another West Coast team, this one in his own conference, was becoming a basketball powerhouse.

The University of California at Berkeley, or "Cal" as the school is known, had a respectable basketball program in the 1940s and early 1950s. But starting with the 1956–57 season, the Cal Golden Bears became the Pacific Coast's "golden team." Under coach Pete

Newell, Cal won four straight conference titles and twice reached the NCAA's championship game, winning the national title in 1959 and taking runner-up honors to Ohio State University in 1960.

During that same four-year period UCLA not only failed to get into the tournament, but steadily faltered in the win category. After going 22–4 in 1956–57, the team posted a mediocre 16–10 record the next year, an equally mediocre 16–9 record the following year, and a disappointing 14–12 record in 1959–60—Wooden's worst since taking over as Bruin coach. A number of UCLA's defeats that year were by slim margins. But as Wooden readily conceded, "We were playing basketball, not horseshoes, so close didn't count."

Too much of a competitor to tolerate the downward spiral, Wooden resolved after that season to make changes. In his campus office, a cramped, unadorned space not much bigger than a cloakroom, he began analyzing all aspects of his basketball program, from how hard he worked his players to how well he substituted them in games to how effectively he recruited. He knew the obvious: "Something was missing. Something was wrong. . . . We were not making as much progress as we should."

UCLA's athletic department wasn't making much progress either. The campus basketball arena Wooden had been promised years earlier remained just that—a promise, nothing more.

12

"The athlete who says that something cannot be done
should never interrupt the one who is doing it."

As John Wooden worked through his frustrations about his
team's performance in 1960, good news arrived from Springfield,
Massachusetts. The Basketball Hall of Fame, located on the campus
of Springfield College, announced that Wooden was to be inducted
for his achievements as a player. The prestigious organization,
today known as the Naismith Memorial Basketball Hall of Fame,
had been established just a year earlier, and its inaugural class
of inductees had included such luminaries as basketball founder
James Naismith and University of Kansas coaching legend Forrest
"Phog" Allen.

Joining Wooden in 1960 in the second and newest class of
basketball elites were other Hoosiers. Former Indiana University
star Emmett "Branch" McCracken and former Purdue University
standout Charles "Stretch" Murphy had their names enshrined
as outstanding players. Wooden's college mentor, Ward "Piggy"
Lambert, was named a Hall of Fame coach.

The honor came too late for Wooden to share with his mother,
Roxie. She had died of heart problems the previous August, and
as he had done at his father's passing, Wooden had gathered with
his brothers for her burial in Centerton Cemetery. At the time
of Roxie's death in 1959, none of her four sons—all of whom

had graduated from college and launched successful careers in
education—resided in Morgan County. Maurice, the oldest,
lived near Wooden in California. Daniel lived in New Mexico and
William lived in La Porte, Indiana.

  After spending much of the off-season reevaluating his
coaching methods, Wooden launched the 1960–61 campaign
with a new practice plan. He split his squad of fifteen players
into two units and put them through scrimmages designed to

*As the rest of the UCLA team looks on, Wooden outlines strategy to his
starters during a game in the 1963–64 season. "The main ingredient of
stardom," Wooden stressed, "is the rest of the team."*

better integrate substitutes and to help the entire squad meld. The revamped practices also cut down on daily "game-type" contact so that, as Wooden explained, "Hopefully, this would stretch [players'] endurance down to those rigorous days of NCAA title play when they would need more energy, drive, and desire."

The new practice regimen appeared to work. The Bruins improved to 18–8 that year, suggesting that UCLA's program was once again on the upswing. But the following autumn, as sportswriters and coaches buzzed about exceptional basketball talent across the nation and as *Sports Illustrated* declared that 1961–62 "should be the finest collegiate season in the 70 years of this feverishly followed sport," no one touted UCLA. The Bruins had no starters taller than six feet, five inches; their 250-pound sophomore center, Fred Slaughter, needed to lose thirty pounds; and their showboating sophomore guard, Walt Hazzard, threw passes his teammates could not catch. As summarized by *Sports Illustrated*: "The Bruins had no height, no center, no muscle, no poise, no experience, no substitutes, and no chance."

UCLA seemed determined to prove the sportswriters correct. It lost seven of its first ten games and looked not tough enough "to mash a mango," according to one sportswriter. But as the weeks went by, Slaughter shed pounds, players learned to catch Hazzard's sizzling passes, and the team drew exceptionally close. A trip to segregated Houston, Texas, where Wooden's racially integrated team experienced hostility on the basketball court, helped cement the Bruins' esprit de corps. After seeing his black players subjected to rough treatment in the first night's game against the University of Houston, Wooden did not play them the second night against Texas A&M University. "It was a silent protest," said then-senior Pete Blackman, recalling how Wooden stood up for the squad's African American players, who also had been refused accommodations in the city's hotels. "It's a tough story to tell and fully comprehend. All I know is that . . . [Wooden's action] welded that ball club together in an extraordinary way," said Blackman.

Displaying both grit and unexpected poise, the Bruins dominated the rest of the season. They won twelve of fourteen games, claimed the conference title, and proved what Wooden had said of his team in December: "We're not actually as bad as we look." UCLA returned to the NCAA tournament after a five-year absence, raring to "mash" more than mangos. But with the school's history of tanking in the first round of regionals, even the Bruin faithful wondered if their team could advance.

Wooden's squad quickly answered the doubters. After defeating Utah State University (73–62) and then Oregon State University (88–69), the Bruins headed to their first-ever Final Four, where they faced off against the University of Cincinnati, the defending national champion. The semifinal battle proved to be a thriller, and the score was tied near the game's end. But with just seconds remaining, Cincinnati squeaked by on a long jump shot to win 72–70. "I have never been more proud of a winning team than I was of this team, even in losing," Wooden said later, referencing how far the "Cinderella" Bruins had advanced that season. For fans, the season sparked hope that a once forgettable basketball program was finally on track to not just chase a national title, but to actually win one. The unanswered question was "when?"

Resolving not to remain completely set in his ways, Wooden made other coaching adjustments as the 1960s unfolded. Recognizing the need to bolster recruiting (something he still found distasteful and refused to sacrifice family time to do), he began assigning scouting duties to a new assistant, Jerry Norman. The personable but brash Norman had played for Wooden in the early 1950s, though the two had often tangled. Norman had been kicked off the team once for using profanity, with Wooden reinstating him only after he apologized. "There were some who wondered about my logic in hiring Jerry, but they didn't know him as I did. He had fine basketball sense and was an excellent recruiter," Wooden said years later.

The two had patched up differences in the mid-1950s when Wooden recommended Norman to coach basketball at nearby

Wooden stands by the Pyramid of Success he developed that covered such areas as friendship, loyalty, self-control, skill, team spirit, poise, confidence, and competitive greatness. Standing with him is UCLA assistant coach Jerry Norman, who recruited many talented Bruins.

West Covina High School, where Maurice Wooden was principal. By the late 1950s Norman was back at UCLA coaching the freshmen team and increasingly earning Wooden's respect. In addition, Norman began tracking down highly talented players and persuading them to attend UCLA—players to whom Wooden was glad to give a uniform.

Norman had another forte besides recruiting. He was a good strategist, and in the spring of 1962, following UCLA's appearance in the Final Four, he urged Wooden to take a fresh approach in the upcoming season. The Bruins were gaining three highly touted newcomers—Gail Goodrich, Keith Erickson, and Jack Hirsch—and Norman believed that the team's quickness and size would lend itself well to a pressure defense, specifically the zone press. Wooden had used the press while at South Bend Central High School and Indiana State Teachers College, but rarely at UCLA, believing that most college players could figure out how to elude it.

Contrary to Wooden's belief, most college players were not savvy enough to stay calm when trapped by a stifling press defense. By the early 1960s, numerous college coaches had concluded as much and were instituting the press to rattle opponents. In February 1962, *Sports Illustrated* declared that the press—"the big weapon for top teams"—had become "the most exciting and exasperating maneuver in basketball."

On Norman's advice, Wooden taught the press to his young team starting in the fall of 1962. While the Bruins did not always execute it perfectly, they began to get results—UCLA scoring attacks from which opponents could not recover. The Bruins finished the year with twenty wins and again advanced to the NCAA Regionals. But red-hot Arizona State University, which used its own version of the press, crushed the Bruins, 93–79. Back on campus, Wooden and Norman plotted how to use the press even more effectively the next year.

Meanwhile, Wooden got a new boss that summer of 1963. J. D. Morgan, UCLA's highly successful men's tennis coach, replaced Wilbur Johns as athletic director. Wooden wasted no time letting Morgan know what he needed, what he had long been promised, and what was in UCLA's best interest—a new basketball arena. Morgan and Chancellor Franklin Murphy agreed to make the project a priority, and soon Los Angeles architect Welton Becket was drafting plans for a state-of-the-art auditorium— half underground, half above-ground—that would seat 12,800 spectators for basketball and other events. The State of California agreed to put up some money for the $5 million project, and a fund-raising campaign was launched. A wealthy California businessman and philanthropist, Indianapolis native Edwin W. Pauley, pledged to donate money equal to what the campaign raised.

With finer facilities finally in the offing, Wooden welcomed back an experienced Bruin team in the fall of 1963. The returnees included all five starters—Hazzard, Slaughter, Goodrich, Erickson, and Hirsch—as well as a talented supporting cast. The starting squad's average height was only six feet, three inches, making UCLA the shortest team in its conference that year. But the starters all possessed raw athletic talent, and Wooden intended to compensate for the team's small size by making use of his players' long arms, quick hands, and fast feet. Wooden and Norman were also committed to using the zone press, fine-tuning it so that the Bruins would sow disharmony among their opponents, leading to turnovers, deflections, and interceptions.

While small size defined the 1963–64 Bruin starters, so did the players' dissimilar backgrounds and ethnicity. Slaughter, an African American, arrived at UCLA from Kansas, where he had been a standout high school athlete in basketball and track. Hazzard, an African American whose father was a preacher, had learned to play basketball in the schoolyards of inner-city Philadelphia. Hirsch, the son of a wealthy Jewish family, had spent much of his youth in Brooklyn before moving to California, where he cruised about in his red Pontiac Grand Prix.

Goodrich and Erickson were the two homegrown West Coasters. Goodrich's father had played basketball for the University of Southern California in the late 1930s, but when that school was slow to show an interest, young Goodrich jumped at the chance to play for Wooden. Erickson was an unabashed beach lover, devoted to surfing and playing volleyball. His volleyball skills were good enough to land him a spot on the U.S. team that competed in the 1964 Olympics in Tokyo.

Temperamentally, the Bruin starters were also as different as their backgrounds. To mold them into a playing unit and to get the most production from each player, Wooden applied principles of human psychology gleaned from his years of experience. He barked at Hazzard, eased up on Goodrich, and put up with a certain amount of horseplay from Erickson. He also learned to bite his tongue around Hirsch, who called him "John" or "J. W." to his face. "In my early years, I wouldn't have tolerated [Hirsch's] informality, but by this time I somehow felt that if it made Jack feel good, what was the harm?" Wooden asked.

Off the court the Bruin starters rarely spent much time together. But in Wooden's presence, they cohered, aware of a special chemistry. "We used to talk about how we were the All-American team, such a group of guys from diverse backgrounds, yet on the court were a perfect mesh," Slaughter recalled years later. "Two black, two white, one Jewish, who after games would go in our separate directions. But game time, practice time, ride-the-bus time, we were pretty well-matched. We liked to protect each other. We liked to do our jobs. And we just enjoyed playing for [Wooden]."

And play they did. Despite failing to make the Top 20 in *Sports Illustrated's* preseason review, the Bruins came on strong. They smashed the school's scoring record by obliterating Brigham Young University 113–71 in their opener. More victories followed, and

The 1963–64 UCLA starting five walk on the Janss Steps, the original entrance to the campus. From left to right: Gail Goodrich, Keith Erickson, Fred Slaughter, Jack Hirsch, and Walt Hazzard.

the Bruins climbed in the polls just as the nation, still shaken by
President John F. Kennedy's assassination in November 1963,
struggled to climb out of its deep mourning. Two days after
Christmas the Bruins decisively beat the vaunted University of
Michigan, 98–80. "The best performance in a single game I've ever
seen by a college team," said University of Illinois coach Harry
Combes, who scouted UCLA that night. By January, the once-
underrated Bruins sat atop the polls.

They stayed there, finishing the regular season with a perfect
26–0 record. Along the way, they dazzled spectators and flummoxed
opponents, who had never seen the zone press—UCLA's trademark
2-2-1 version—so flawlessly executed and with such dramatic
results. Sportswriters began applying terms such as "The Glue
Factory" and "Arranged Chaos" to UCLA's suffocating defense. USC
coach Forrest Twogood offered his own take on what it was like to
play against the Bruin press: "Have you ever been locked up in a
casket for six days? That's how it feels."

Although UCLA entered the NCAA tournament undefeated,
sportswriters doubted the Bruins would go the distance. In
tournament history only two teams, the University of San
Francisco and the University of North Carolina, had managed to
extend their perfect records through to the championship game.
True to form, the Bruins nearly ended their season in the first
round of regionals. Trailing late in the game, they barely beat
Seattle University, 95–90. The next night they trailed San Francisco
at halftime, but then mounted their famous "Blitz" to win 76–72.

At the Final Four in Kansas City's aging Municipal Auditorium,
the Bruins faced Kansas State University, a team UCLA had
narrowly defeated in December. Determined to avenge that loss,

the Wildcats played aggressively and, buoyed by the cheers of home-crowd fans, led by five points with barely seven minutes remaining in the game. But the Bruins fought back to a 75–75 tie and then received some unexpected moral support. UCLA's cheerleaders, their arrival delayed by a snowstorm, came rushing into the auditorium just as their team mounted a swift scoring attack. The Bruins put the game away, 90–84, and then headed to where they had never been before—the tourney final.

Duke University, which had bested Michigan in the semifinals, was heavily favored to win the national title. A commanding team at both ends of the court, Duke had All-American forward and eventual National Basketball Association All-Star Jeff Mullins and two six-foot-ten-inch players, Hack Tison and Jay Buckley. "If you are silly enough to apply logic to basketball, there's no way for UCLA to beat Duke," the *Kansas City Star's* Dick Wade wrote on the eve of the championship. "The Blue Devils simply have too much—height, rebounding, shooting ability and defense."

Wooden was well aware of his team's underdog status. He recalled sitting in the lobby of Kansas City's Muehlebach Hotel hours before the big game and bristling at comments made by passersby: "'Nice try, Wooden' was what I sensed. . . .The [Bruins] were still viewed as almost lucky to be in the finals. This burned me up."

The real burning, however, took place on the basketball court. UCLA trailed Duke 30–27 late in the first half and looked to be in trouble as Erickson picked up his third foul. But then the Bruins, heeding Wooden's advice to be patient and stick with their pressure defense, broke Duke's tempo, launched a blistering blitz, and scored sixteen unanswered points in under three minutes to take a 43–30 lead. The shaken Blue Devils never recovered as the Bruins swarmed

Wooden and his team celebrate winning the national championship over Duke University in 1964. Players in front row are, from left to right: Goodrich, Hazzard, and Hirsch, holding trophy.

and harassed, chased and intercepted, outran and outrebounded them. UCLA forced twenty-nine turnovers and made enough quick baskets in transition to coast to a 98–83 victory. "They led us early, but it only took us two or three minutes to catch up," said Wooden later. "But the lead wasn't the thing. It was the look they had on their faces. They looked whipped."

The victory was number thirty for UCLA in a perfect season, and by coincidence it came on the thirtieth birthday of Wooden's daughter, Nan. Starting before Nan's birth, Wooden had been trying to lead a team to a state or national championship and in the intervening years had suffered through his share of near misses. "You are champions," he told his players that March night in 1964. "And you must act like champions. You met some people going up to the top. You will meet the same people going down."

At age fifty-three and with his first NCAA winners' wristwatch in hand, Wooden had no immediate plans for going down.

13

*"Consider the rights of others before your own feelings
and the feelings of others before your own rights."*

When folk artist Bob Dylan released his hit song "The Times
They Are a-Changin'" in 1964, change was easy to spot throughout
America. A country that had prided itself on winning World
War II was venturing into an unwinnable war in Southeast Asia.
African Americans' fight for racial equality was leading to both
new legislation and social upheaval. And a youth-driven society,
aroused from the relative tranquility of the 1950s, was beginning
to experiment with drugs, embrace long hair and loud music, and
thumb its nose at "old ways."

Change was also on display at UCLA. Campus buildings were
springing up, new schools and institutes were being established,
and enrollment—exceeding 20,000 students—continued to
climb. Westwood, home to Hollis Johnson's drugstore where John
Wooden regularly lunched on deviled-egg sandwiches, was still just
a village next to campus. But skyscrapers, pricey condominiums,
and upscale businesses would soon transform the village, signaling
even more change.

Fresh off his national championship, Wooden had demonstrated
he was willing to reconsider some of his long-held coaching beliefs.
Even so, as he welcomed his team to practice in the fall of 1964, his
"tried and true" ways were very much in evidence. He still handed

out copies of his "Pyramid of Success" and demonstrated how to
pull up socks and lace shoes (even as many players rolled their
eyes). He still called out the day's drills from three-inch-by-five-
inch index cards on file from previous years. He still emphasized
conditioning, fundamentals, and teamwork.

The 1964–65 season opened in the University of Illinois's
new Assembly Hall, where the sharpshooting Fighting Illini
demolished the Bruins and ran up the highest score ever on a
UCLA team, 110–83. "It was no fluke. We got slashed to bits,"
Wooden recalled. Even so, he told his team the next day not to
worry, reminding them that the pressure of their thirty-game
winning streak was over. "Just go out and play your game," player
Freddie Goss remembered Wooden saying.

Their jitters eased, the Bruins lost only one other contest
the rest of the regular season before resuming their march
through the NCAA tournament. They eliminated Brigham Young
University, the University of San Francisco, and Wichita State
University to again reach the final game, and this time their
opponent was the University of Michigan, ranked Number One
in the nation and loaded with heavyweights such as eventual
National Basketball Association star Cazzie Russell. "I doubt if any
team in the pro ranks is bigger or stronger. There certainly are no
thin men out there," Wooden said of the Wolverines.

But if the Bruins seemed scrawny by comparison, they did not
play puny. After Michigan took an early lead, UCLA unleashed its
explosive weapon—the zone press—and eventually took control,
leading by as many as twenty points in the second half. Gail
Goodrich scored forty-two points, breaking a school record, and
Kenny Washington came off the bench to add seventeen points.

The final score was 91–80, giving Wooden and the Bruins their second national title and making UCLA the fifth team in NCAA history to win back-to-back championships.

As sweet as that victory was, sweet news of another kind reached Wooden several weeks later. On May 4, 1965, Ferdinand Lewis Alcindor Jr., a seven-foot high-school sensation from New York City, announced that he planned to attend UCLA and play for the Bruins. His announcement ended months of speculation, with coaches around the country offering him scholarships and with Michigan, Saint John's University, College of the Holy Cross, and Boston College doing their best to woo him.

Alcindor, who later changed his name to Kareem Abdul-Jabbar, was a blue-chip prospect if ever there was one. A four-year varsity player at an all-boys Catholic school in Manhattan, Alcindor was a prep All-American by his sophomore year and helped lead Power Memorial Academy to seventy-one consecutive victories over three seasons. He was smart, agile, unselfish with the ball, and in full command of his great height. "Lewis was one of a kind," recalled Wooden. "I hadn't really expected to get him."

Alcindor's high school coach, Jack Donohue, had recommended his star center to Wooden. The two coaches had met the previous summer at a Philadelphia basketball clinic, and after listening to Donohue talk about "his big fellow," Wooden said he was definitely interested. But Wooden had one request: He asked that the high school senior visit UCLA last.

Alcindor obliged and waited until early April 1965, after UCLA had just won its second championship, to visit the Westwood campus. After meeting with Wooden and then getting a Los Angeles-area tour that included Hollywood and lavish doses of

California sunshine, Alcindor verbally committed to UCLA. Soon afterward, Alcindor asked Wooden to come to New York to meet his parents. This time Wooden obliged, meeting with the family after midnight because that was when Alcindor's father, a transit policeman, got off work.

Accompanied by assistant coach Jerry Norman, Wooden spoke to Cora and Ferdinand Sr. for about an hour. He emphasized UCLA's high academic standing and assured them their son would receive a good education. But Wooden, aware that a continent would separate Alcindor from his home, remained skeptical as to whether the recruit would actually enroll. Even after Alcindor formally announced his decision on May 4, Wooden still had his doubts: "I wondered if he would really show up in September for classes."

But he did show up. And his arrival coincided with the opening of UCLA's gleaming new arena, the long-awaited Pauley Pavilion. Dedicated in June, the arena finally gave the Bruin basketball program a permanent campus home. It also meant the team no longer had to climb flights of stairs to practice in a dusty, antiquated gym, sharing the space with wrestlers and gymnasts.

The first game in the new facility was on November 27, 1965. A crowd of more than 12,000 turned out that night for the traditional scrimmage between UCLA's varsity and freshmen squads, and while spectators had plenty to feast their eyes on—the vastness of the new pavilion, the sleek, modern design, the gold-upholstered seats, and the blue-padded bleachers—the real spectacle was on the hardwood. The freshmen team, led by Alcindor, broke the game open early and pummeled the varsity, which sat atop the preseason rankings. Displaying his quickness, poise, and ability to intimidate, Alcindor scored thirty-one points, grabbed twenty-one rebounds, blocked shots, and thwarted the varsity's effort to play their full-court press. The final score was 75–60, leading some fans to quip that UCLA was Number One in the nation but Number Two on its own campus.

As required under NCAA rules at the time, Alcindor remained on the freshmen squad all season and helped the Brubabes, as they were called, go undefeated. Wooden's varsity, meanwhile, struggled throughout the 1965–66 season, hampered by illnesses and injuries and managing only an 18–8 record, which cost the Bruins an NCAA tournament invitation.

Denied the chance to compete that March, UCLA instead watched what proved to be a landmark contest in the tournament's championship game. Texas Western University, a little-known school in remote El Paso, Texas, stunned the college basketball world by having its all-black starting squad defeat the heavily favored, all-white University of Kentucky Wildcats. Coming at the height of the civil-rights era, that victory further hastened racial integration in the sport—so dramatically, in fact, that every foot-dragging Southern Conference opened its doors to black players the following season.

Back in Westwood, UCLA fans awaited the new season with heightened anticipation. The towering New York teenager who wore size sixteen sneakers would be eligible to play varsity in the fall. And with Alcindor in the lineup, oddsmakers were already wagering Wooden's squad would be unstoppable.

* * * *

Alcindor was not the only college player of great height at the start of the 1966–67 season. Fifty collegians stood roughly seven feet tall, including the University of Southern California's Ron

Taylor. But when Alcindor took the floor against USC in his first varsity game that December, he brought more to center court than just his size. Displaying strength as well as agility, he scored fifty-six points, a school record, to lead the Bruins to an easy win over their archrival. Soon afterward, on consecutive nights against Duke University, he scored a total of fifty-seven points, prompting Duke coach Vic Bubas to say, "He destroys you, that's what he does."

To take full advantage of Alcindor's height (UCLA listed him as seven feet one and a half inches tall), Wooden designed a new team offense prior to the season. He assigned Alcindor to the "low post," a position near the basket and well inside the free throw line. "I almost wanted him to be able to stick his arm out and dunk the ball—no more than eight feet away," said Wooden. To assist his star player, Wooden tapped the defensive talents and superlative shooting of three other sophomores—Lynn Shackelford, Kenny Heitz, and Lucius Allen. For experience, Wooden looked to junior Mike Warren, a playmaking guard from a familiar place, Central High School in South Bend, Indiana.

A two-time Hoosier All-State player, Warren was uncertain in the spring of 1964 where he would attend college. Though he had numerous scholarship offers, UCLA was not in the mix until one day his geometry teacher, Walt Kindy, mentioned that he was a friend of Wooden's. Kindy, who had assisted Wooden in his coaching days at Central, offered to place a call to Los Angeles. Endorsing that idea was Jim Powers, who at the time was coaching Warren and who himself had played for Wooden at Central and at Indiana State Teachers College.

After a visit to UCLA was hastily arranged, Warren met the coach who had just won his first national championship. But the

Left to right: Lew Alcindor (as he was then known; he later changed his name to Kareem Abdul-Jabbar), Mike Warren, and Wooden prepare for the 1967–68 basketball season. Looking back on Wooden's influence, Abdul-Jabbar noted that Wooden "taught us that the best you are capable of is victory enough, and that you can't walk until you crawl, that gentle but profound truth about growing up."

COURTESY INDIANA BASKETBALL HALL OF FAME

Inducted into the Indiana Basketball Hall of Fame in 1992, Warren became an actor after the end of his playing career.

meeting in Wooden's plainly furnished office in "an awful pea-green colored building" was not what the young recruit expected: "Okay, new [UCLA] offices were being constructed but heck, his team had just won . . . basketball's biggest prize and he had been selected 'Coach of the Year.' I had expected to see all the trappings of that undefeated season, even in a temporary setting. There were none."

Neither was there boasting. Warren recalled that Wooden "never once mentioned the championship." Equally surprisingly, or so it seemed to Warren at the time, was Wooden's instruction that the young Hoosier must graduate from whatever college he selected. "What college coach has the nerve to talk about making graduating the goal even if the player elected to go elsewhere?" asked Warren.

Wooden's trademark soft sell worked to good effect, with Warren never regretting his decision to head west. He was a three-year varsity starter at UCLA, and after college he launched a successful acting career, playing the role of policeman Bobby Hill on the 1980s Emmy-winning television series *Hill Street Blues*. During the 1966–67 basketball season, however, the role Warren performed most skillfully was that of Wooden's floor general—the savvy leader responsible for molding his mates into a cohesive whole. "He was as smart and valuable a guard as I ever had," Wooden said of Warren.

As the basketball pundits had predicted, UCLA barreled over its opponents and finished the regular season undefeated. Returning to the NCAA tournament in March 1967, the Bruins charged past three teams and then defeated the University of Dayton by a 79–64 score for the championship. That win gave them their third NCAA crown, a number matched only by the University of Kentucky. Wooden also moved into a league of his own, becoming the first coach with two perfect seasons (30–0 in 1964 and in 1967).

A third perfect season and another national championship
seemed highly likely for the Bruins the following year. With
UCLA's five starters, including Alcindor, back, the Bruins looked
to be as formidable as ever, and opposing coaches everywhere
plotted how to knock them off their pedestal. The first test of
UCLA's invincibility came in early December 1967. Wooden took
his squad to West Lafayette, Indiana, for a season opener against
his alma mater.

The hoopla-laden game christened Purdue University's new $6
million arena and marked the varsity debut of Boilermaker Rick
Mount, who was Indiana's Mr. Basketball in 1966 and the first
high school team athlete to grace the cover of *Sports Illustrated*.
More than 14,000 fans turned out to see if Mount and his
teammates could upset Wooden's national champions. Showing
up, too, were hordes of writers, photographers, radio broadcasters,
and television cameramen, leading *Sports Illustrated* to declare:
"With all the clickety-clacking, whirring, play-by-play yakking,
band music and cheering, it was a wonder John Purdue [the
college's namesake] didn't wake up in his grave."

Though he played with an injured foot, Mount scored twenty-
eight points that night, and his teammates performed equally
well, forcing Bruin turnovers and preventing Alcindor from
getting passes. The Boilermakers played UCLA to a 71–71 tie,
but in the frantic closing seconds UCLA backup guard Bill Sweek
sank a basket, and UCLA's win record remained intact. Still, a near
upset in his former backyard did not please Wooden, as then U.S.
Senator Birch Bayh Jr. discovered when he poked his head into
the Bruin locker room. The senator and Purdue alum had gone to
the locker room to extend some Hoosier hospitality to the UCLA

WIKIPEDIA COMMONS

During his career at Purdue University, All-American Rick Mount led his team to an overall record of 56–20 and held for a time the Big Ten's all-time scoring record.

coach. But when Bayh came upon a red-faced Wooden scolding his players, he made a hasty exit. "I said my hello and good-bye and welcome to Indiana in one breath," Bayh recalled. "I knew I had to get out of there."

All the media attention lavished on the UCLA-Purdue matchup was nothing compared to the hype the following month. In a January 1968 contest that promoters billed as "The Game of the Century," UCLA played the University of Houston in that city's mammoth Astrodome. Nearly 53,000 spectators attended the game—the largest crowd ever to witness a basketball contest. It also was the first regular-season game ever to be nationally televised.

At the time, UCLA had stretched its winning streak to forty-seven games and was ranked Number One in the country. Ranked Number Two, the Houston Cougars boasted a long-running winning streak at home, and they also had their own self-assured superstar, six-foot-eight-inch Elvin Hayes, or, as the media called him, the "Big E." Hayes was confident he could overpower UCLA's "Big Lew," and at game time his confidence seemed well placed. Alcindor was suffering from a scratched cornea, the result of getting poked in the eye eight days earlier, and his performance in the dome was not up to par. He made only four of eighteen shots while Hayes played sensationally, scoring thirty-nine points, grabbing fifteen rebounds, and in the final half minute hitting two free throws to win the game, 71–69.

In what was already a carnival-like atmosphere, pandemonium broke out at center court as Houston fans celebrated. Their team had humbled the mighty Bruins and handed Alcindor his first loss since high school. Wooden took the loss in stride. But rabid UCLA fans were not as forgiving. When Wooden addressed the Bruin Hoopsters booster group the following week, fans aggressively second-guessed his game strategy. "You should have seen what they put that poor man through," said a Wooden loyalist who attended.

Wooden's wife, Nell, pays a quick visit to the UCLA bench during a 1968 game against the University of Oregon.

The cover photograph on the next issue of *Sports Illustrated* did not ease Bruin fans' discontent. The photo showed Hayes shooting over Alcindor's up-stretched arm, with the headline "Big EEEE Over Big Lew." Said Alcindor: "I took that cover and taped it up to my locker."

The Bruins did not lose another game the rest of the regular season, and as fate would have it, they met up with Houston in the NCAA semifinals. As fate would also have it, this game was played in friendlier Bruin territory, the Los Angeles Sports Arena. With Alcindor fully recovered and with UCLA hungry for revenge, the Bruins used a new "diamond-and-one" zone defense to limit Hayes to the lowest point total (ten) of his college career. At one point, UCLA was ahead by forty-four points and if Wooden had not sent in substitute players in the closing five minutes, the devastation might have been worse. As it was, the Bruins demolished the undefeated Cougars, 101–69. "That was the greatest exhibition of basketball I've ever seen," Houston coach Guy Lewis said afterward.

The following night, the Bruins managed another rout. They defeated the University of North Carolina 78–55 for their fourth championship in five years. UCLA also became the only team to win back-to-back national titles twice, in 1964 and 1965 and in 1967 and 1968. But even as Alcindor and Warren were cutting down the nets and draping them around their necks, and even as the big NCAA trophy was being presented, basketball buffs were already thinking about next year. Could the Bruins make history by winning three championships in a row? "It's difficult to do, very difficult," said a realistic Wooden.

14

*"Ability may get you to the top, but it takes
character to keep you there."*

With Lew Alcindor returning to play his senior year, John
Wooden knew what everyone else knew—UCLA's dominance
of college basketball would likely continue in the 1968–69
season. But "dominance" did not guarantee another national
championship, and Wooden wrestled over how to ward off player
complacency and make sure, as he put it, "that the infection of
success didn't set in to spoil" the team's chances.

Trouble surfaced early. In the spring of 1968, UCLA's
lightning-fast starting guard Lucius Allen abruptly quit school. A
self-described rebel, he dropped out because of academic troubles
and around the same time that his second arrest on marijuana-
possession charges became public. Allen had been arrested the
previous spring, but those charges were soon dropped due to
insufficient evidence. Following his second arrest, he was placed
on one-year probation and fined $300.

Wooden considered Allen, who eventually became a National
Basketball Association star and expressed regret for his reckless
behavior in college, to have been an exceptionally gifted guard,
especially when paired with Mike Warren. "One of the greatest
guard combines . . . that I have ever coached," Wooden said of
the two young men. But great as they had been, they were now

gone, Warren having graduated that spring. The bottom line for Wooden—his backcourt lineup was unsettled.

The nation was also unsettled in 1968. College campuses, UCLA's among them, roiled as students and faculty increasingly staged rallies, marches, and sit-ins to protest the Vietnam War. Outside of academia, turmoil took other forms that spring and summer as civil-rights leader Martin Luther King Jr. and presidential candidate Robert F. Kennedy were slain, rioting spread across cities, and violence broke out at the Democratic National Convention in Chicago.

Even the 1968 Olympic Games, which took place in October in Mexico City, were embroiled in controversy. African American athletes, seeking to protest the treatment of blacks in the United States, had talked about boycotting the Olympics. A "Black Power" boycott never materialized, but two black sprinters on the U.S. Olympic team made an overtly political statement

Demonstrators protest outside of the White House after the assassination of Martin Luther King Jr. in April 1968.

during the medal-award ceremony. They raised a dark-gloved fist aloft, bowed their heads, and refused to look at the American flag during the playing of the national anthem—behavior that infuriated many and became front-page news around the world.

Alcindor had his own brush with that controversy. He had attended a meeting the previous November where the possibility of a boycott was discussed. When the media learned of his attendance, he was besieged with questions, as was UCLA's athletic department. Though Alcindor remained uncommitted as to whether he would compete in the Olympics, critics called him ugly names, flooded him with hate mail, and accused him of being a traitor for not wanting to help the U.S. basketball team win a gold medal. Some said he should be thrown out of UCLA and barred from professional basketball; others vowed never to watch another game until he was gone.

In the end, Alcindor chose not to compete, his reasons being, among others, that he did not want to disrupt his academic studies. (A high-achieving, independent-thinking history major, Alcindor finished in four years and later took classes at Harvard University.) Wooden, meanwhile, steered clear of interfering, saying early on in the boycott controversy that "how a player of mine feels about society is his own business, whether he's black, yellow, or white." Alcindor later acknowledged the lack of interference: "I'll give UCLA credit: The school never brought a bit of pressure on me, never remotely suggested that I should shut up or refuse to discuss controversial issues."

As they had the previous fall, the Bruins opened their season playing Purdue University. This time the game was at Pauley Pavilion, instead of in West Lafayette, Indiana, and again the Bruins won, though by a comfortable twelve-point margin instead of a squeaker at the buzzer. Two road games followed at Ohio State University and the University of Notre Dame, and, as Alcindor later recounted, the late-night bus ride between the two schools helped to set the tone for the season.

Bruin players—among them a devout Protestant, a Catholic, and a Jew—were talking aboard the bus about religion when Alcindor announced that he had recently converted from Catholicism to Islam. Initially, he recalled, "there was a hush." But then the discussion resumed, and, as Alcindor further recounted, "nobody seemed to care that I was a Muslim. They accepted it and we talked about it. The world did not come to an end. Coach Wooden did not look at me cross-eyed. He seemed to accept it as well as everybody else. Out of that midnight ride across Ohio and

Wooden watches his UCLA team's performance in a March 7, 1969, game against the Bruins' archrival, the University of Southern California. "A coach is someone," he noted, "who can give correction without causing resentment."

Indiana we became a different group of men, much more than just a bunch of jocks traveling around the country bouncing basketballs."

Piling easy victory upon victory, the Bruins rode a 25–1 record into the NCAA tournament, helped by John Vallely, the junior-college transfer who Wooden had found for his backcourt. UCLA's only loss in the regular season, and its first ever defeat in Pauley Pavilion, came right before the tournament when the University of Southern California pulled off a 46–44 upset. Regrouping quickly, the Bruins easily knocked off opponents in the tournament's regionals and survived a close contest in the semifinals. They again faced Purdue, this time in Louisville, Kentucky, for the 1969 national championship.

UCLA guard Kenny Heitz was assigned to stop "The Rocket," the Boilermakers' Rick Mount, and with his long, wispy arms Heitz did just that. The usually sure-shooting Mount hit only twelve of thirty-six shots and missed fourteen in a row. As superbly as Heitz, Vallely, and other Bruins performed, however, Alcindor's showing was even better, "brilliant" in the words of *Sports Illustrated*. In the final game of his college career, Alcindor scored thirty-seven points, grabbed twenty rebounds, and led UCLA to a 92–72 drubbing of Purdue. Among those cheering Alcindor was his father, playing trombone that day in the Bruin band.

Had the NCAA not outlawed the dunk shot after Alcindor's sophomore year (his mastery of the shot prompted the ban), his UCLA career might have been even more spectacular. As it was, Alcindor still earned the game's highest honors throughout his varsity years, and at that year's tournament, he became, and remains, the only man to be named the "Most Outstanding Player" three times.

UCLA also claimed the number "three" that day—three straight NCAA titles, an achievement matched by no other school. Wooden claimed another number: five national titles in six years, more than any other college coach. He had leaped ahead of the University of Kentucky's Adolph Rupp, who had four.

"I've heard it said that any coach would have won championships with Lewis. That might be true, it really might," said Wooden after the game. But Kareem Abdul-Jabbar, the Muslim name that Alcindor adopted after his graduation and by which he was known in his long and illustrious National Basketball Association career, reflected years later on what it takes to win a championship, and he declined to personally accept too much credit. Instead he

Wooden and his wife, Nell, are joined by their children, Jim and Nan, during a 1969 visit to the Fall Foliage Festival in Martinsville, Indiana.

praised his former coach. "In order to win a championship, you have to have a lot of parts that fit together, and you have to have the opportunity to win," said the former Bruin star. "I think the reason that UCLA's teams did so well was that Coach Wooden's ideas on unity and team play really were cutting edge and the best. He taught those elements of the game the best of any coach in the country. You combine that with talented athletes and you're going to have a winning program."

In the weeks and months after the 1969 championship, Wooden, his name and program now synonymous with excellence, hauled in more honors. Sportswriters again named him "College Basketball Coach of the Year," his third such award from United Press International. His church denomination, Disciples of Christ, named him "Outstanding Basketball Coach of the U.S." And in October he returned by invitation to Martinsville, Indiana, whereupon the city named a street after him, the mayor presented him with a gift, and townsfolk cheered as he—parade grand marshal for Morgan County's annual Fall Foliage Festival—rode past in a convertible. A Martinsville newspaper noted on the eve of the festivities: "Local people swell up like prideful toads at the mere mention of his name—and the greater the friendship, the bigger the swell."

Hurrying back to Westwood for the start of a new season, Wooden began assembling his "Team Without." The label was his, and though it referred to the absence of Alcindor, it was not meant as an insult. Wooden sensed that his players wanted to prove they could win without the tall superstar. Wooden felt likewise: "It will be fun coaching to win again, rather than coaching to try to keep from losing."

Though the Bruins lacked a towering center, they did not lack for experience. Two starters, senior guard Vallely and junior forward Curtis Rowe, were back, as was junior Sidney Wicks, who had come off the bench to play forward the previous year. New to the mix was sophomore guard Henry Bibby, who had learned to make long arching shots while growing up on a tiny North Carolina tobacco farm. Playing center was junior Steve Patterson, who as a redshirt had had to body up daily in practice against Alcindor. Wooden returned to coaching them in the style he was most comfortable—a high-post, running offense. As in earlier days, the Bruins were also taught to press.

The "Team Without" wasted no time proving itself. It lost only two games during the regular season, and by March it was back in the NCAA tournament—and back in the championship game. The Bruins squared off against Jacksonville University, the nation's tallest team with a front line that included seven-foot-two-inch Artis Gilmore. Nicknamed "Batman," Gilmore was a premier shot blocker. But against the quickness and poise of the Bruins, and especially the intimidating defense of Wicks, known for his fearsome glare, Gilmore shot poorly and even had *his* shots blocked. UCLA won 80–69, its fourth championship in a row and sixth in seven years.

Predictably, Wooden, whose family by then had grown to include grandchildren, received more honors and congratulations. The day after the team's win, he received a phone call that took him by complete surprise:

"The operator said, 'Long distance calling.' I waited and waited and waited. It seemed a long while. The grandchildren were impatient to go, Nellie was waving at me, and [granddaughter] Cathleen was pulling me by the arm. 'Operator,' I said as she came back on the line for a second, 'I'm ready to take my family out to dinner. They are all waiting. If this isn't something important, I'm just going to have to leave. I can't wait any longer.'"

"'Sir,' she said, 'the President of the United States is calling.'"

After stammering that he would wait and wondering if his team might be playing a prank, Wooden heard President Richard Nixon come on the line and say how much he had enjoyed the game. Satisfied that it really was *the* president, Wooden accepted Nixon's well wishes. "A tremendous thrill—a wonderful gesture on his part," Wooden said afterward.

The 1969–70 season did not end on all high notes, however. At the team's annual spring banquet, typically a festive affair where the seniors gave their farewell address, reserve player Bill Seibert, who had seen little action as a Bruin, bitterly rapped Wooden and his program. Before a crowd of roughly eight hundred people at the Beverly Hills Hilton, Seibert described his years at UCLA as "an unhappy experience," complained about a "lack of communication" between players and coaches, and accused Wooden of treating starters and substitutes unequally. As Seibert talked on and on, the crowd expressed its

LIBRARY OF CONGRESS

Richard Nixon, the thirty-seventh president of the United States. In 1974 he became the only president to resign from office.

discomfort and outright disgust by booing him, and even Seibert's father yelled at his son to sit down. Seibert's teammates, in turn, gave him a standing ovation. "In a day and age when the common rallying cry at universities across the country was 'power to the people,' Bill had taken his brief moment in the spotlight to question a man who seemed beyond reproach," teammate Andy Hill said later, recalling the evening. "Though many on the team disagreed with Bill's timing and choice of venue, we all admired his courage."

Displaying his usual composure, Wooden gave a gracious response after Seibert's speech and said he was sorry the young man felt as he did. Asked later about Seibert's remarks, Wooden said "the boy took advantage of the situation. I didn't feel it was in good taste or polite or good manners, either." The two had more business to transact. Within days of the banquet, Wooden recommended Seibert for a teaching-coaching fellowship in Australia—a recommendation that Seibert, who later made his peace with the coach, described as "very generous."

Still, the banquet incident was messy. Stung by Seibert's criticism, Wooden met individually with a few players and then with the entire team, where he was informed that players wanted him to be their coach but not control their private lives. They also wanted to feel free to voice their opinions. "You shouldn't feel threatened by this," Bruin leader Wicks told Wooden, his remarks helping to diffuse tension in the room. "We're here as a team. You're the one who taught us to be a team."

But the Bruins were not finished testing Wooden's authority, and they irritated their coach again that spring. Identifying themselves as "UCLA 1970 NCAA Basketball Champions," the team sent a letter to Nixon condemning the Vietnam War and the recent shootings at Kent State University, triggered by student antiwar protests. Hill, who helped craft and circulate the letter, was summoned to hear Wooden's disapproval firsthand. "It would be the height of understatement to say he was not pleased," said Hill, recalling his "chat" with Wooden.

Putting the off-season distractions behind him, Wooden got back to the business that fall of running the basketball team on his terms. Players fell in line, their respect for his coaching skills trumping their own rebelliousness. With workmanlike precision, the Bruins, led by the frontline trio of Wicks, Rowe, and Patterson, hammered out victory after victory in the 1970–71 season. Their momentum was slowed in late January 1971 when the University of Notre Dame pulled off an 89–82 upset, a game in which Austin Carr scored forty-six points to secure the Irish win. Chastened by that nationally televised loss in South Bend, Indiana, the Bruins regained their footing and took a 25–1 record into the NCAA tournament. In short order, they ended up where they wanted to be—in the finals in the Houston Astrodome, pitted this time against Villanova University.

Compared to previous title games, where a UCLA win seemed almost a foregone conclusion, the crowd of 31,400 witnessed a battle to the end. The Bruins led by eleven at the half, but with four minutes remaining the margin shrank to four points, then three, helped by the dazzling play of Villanova's Howard Porter. But UCLA's Patterson, who had turned down two professional offers to play his senior year, performed superbly as well. He scored a career high twenty-nine points to help seal a 68–62 Bruin win and to satisfy all the UCLA fans wearing "Gimme five" buttons. In the college basketball universe, those buttons needed little translation: UCLA had just won its fifth straight NCAA championship and seven of the last eight.

Just seconds before the clock ran out and all the celebrating commenced, the irrepressible Wicks paused long enough to shout, "Coach, you're really something." Wooden, who had had his run-ins with the flamboyant forward, could only smile. That year's team, as well as the one from the previous year, had been special to him. They had proven they could win *without* Alcindor, and that effort gained them, as Wooden said, "my everlasting affection."

Still, the championship frenzy had barely subsided when speculation shifted to UCLA's prospects for the following season. Four of the Bruin starters, including Wicks, were graduating, leading Wooden to tell reporters: "Only a lamebrain would pick us for national honors, with a completely new team." But a redheaded freshman was waiting to join the varsity. And no one, including the sixty-year-old Wooden, was ready to count the Bruins out.

15

"You can't let praise or criticism get to you.
It's a weakness to get caught up in either one."

As John Wooden said good-bye to his seniors in the spring of 1971, he bid another Bruin farewell. His top assistant, Denny Crum, resigned to accept the head coaching job at the University of Louisville. Crum, who played for UCLA in the late 1950s, had been Wooden's right-hand man and chief recruiter since 1968, when Jerry Norman left to become a full-time stockbroker.

Like Norman, Crum was energetic, intense, and not afraid to voice his opinions—qualities Wooden liked in his assistants. But during the semifinal game in Houston, Crum rankled Wooden with advice on substitutions and strategy, and a well-publicized argument ensued. Wooden threatened to banish Crum to the end of the bench and at one point snapped: "I'm the coach of this team, and don't tell me how to coach my team." Coincidentally or not, Crum accepted the Louisville job on April 17.

Wooden replaced Crum with Gary Cunningham, another former Bruin player. Cunningham had been a starting forward on UCLA's first-ever Final Four team in 1962. He had also coached the freshmen squad in 1965 when Lew Alcindor and his teammates embarrassed the varsity. "An exceptional analyst" who had "a very winning way about him" is how Wooden described his new assistant.

When practice began for the 1971–72 season, Wooden had reason to like what he saw. Senior Henry Bibby, the artful shooting guard, was back in uniform as was junior Larry Farmer, a leaping forward who had seen some varsity action the previous year. Returning, too, were bench players who could have been starters at most any other school. But it was the talented sophomore class, with forward Keith Wilkes and guards Greg Lee and Tommy Curtis, that most excited Wooden. And the most promising sophomore was six-foot-eleven-inch Bill Walton, the star recruit who some predicted would be UCLA's next Alcindor.

With his freckles, curly red hair, and long stride, Walton had been easy to spot on campus when he arrived a year earlier. He had come to UCLA from suburban San Diego, California, where he had grown up in a middle-class family, a shy boy who, in his words, "stuttered horrendously." He took up basketball at an early age and was helped by growth spurts, shooting up from six feet one inch to six feet seven inches between his sophomore and junior years of high school, and up to six feet ten inches before his senior year. Along with his height, he possessed quickness. He was also a superb passer.

Recognizing Walton as a top-flight prospect, college coaches flooded him with letters and telephone calls, many offering to take him and his family out to dinner. Walton's father, Ted, turned down those offers. The family did, however, invite a select few to the Walton home for a meal, and Wooden, making one of his few recruiting trips, dined at their table. "You're the player we want. . . . We're not going to promise you that you'll start but we think you can. But you're going to have to earn it," Wooden told the high-school senior, remarks in line with what he typically told recruits.

Walton was already sold on Wooden's fast-break and passing style of play, not to mention UCLA's academic reputation, athletic record, and beautiful campus. Recalling that he had no trouble reaching a decision, Walton said, "For a high school kid growing up at that time, everyone wanted to go to UCLA."

UCLA basketball player Bill Walton, March 15, 1972.

ASSOCIATED PRESS

Walton dominated immediately. He led UCLA's freshmen team to an undefeated season, and as the 1971–72 season kicked off, he took charge vocally, pleasing Wooden with the way he called out "more warnings and advice to his teammates than any player I have ever had." Fans also loved the tall center, especially his enthusiasm, acrobatic moves, and speed. Sportswriters took to calling the Bruins "The Walton Gang," and they duly noted his rookie-year contributions. "Everything UCLA does well stems directly from Walton and his extraordinary talents," declared a *Sports Illustrated* writer. "He is everywhere—tipping in missed shots, leaping out of nowhere for blocks, chasing loose balls, calling the signals for UCLA's 2-2-1 zone press."

After easily winning their first seven games, contests in which they scored more than 100 points per game, the Bruins continued to mow down opponents. They confidently took their 26–0 record into the NCAA tournament and tacked on two more wins in the regionals. In the semifinals Crum arrived with his newly inherited Louisville team, and both he and Wooden teased each other good-naturedly before their two squads took to the floor. But the Bruins made sure Crum did not upstage his former boss. UCLA polished off Louisville 96–77, then went on to beat Florida State, 81–76, for a sixth-straight championship.

With the victory, and another NCAA trophy, the Bruins had achieved a perfect 30–0 record, the third time a Wooden-coached team went undefeated all season. Significantly, the Walton Gang had not just *won* games; throughout the year they had outscored opponents by an average of thirty points a contest. For his contributions, Walton, who averaged twenty-one points a game and shot 64 percent during the season, was named college basketball's Player of the Year. He was also named the tournament's most outstanding player.

While approving Walton's on-court performance, Wooden was less than thrilled with his star's off-court activities. In May 1972, barely a month after the season ended, Walton was arrested for participating in a campus antiwar demonstration prompted by President Richard Nixon's announcement that the United States would mine North Vietnam's harbors. Walton initially joined protestors in a sit-down in the middle of a busy Westwood street. The next two days he joined rallies at which students occupied and barricaded the entrance to Murphy Hall, an administration building. One of dozens of students arrested outside the building, Walton was subsequently fined fifty dollars by a judge. He also was placed on conditional probation by the university for two years. A frustrated Wooden had "words" with Walton, hoping to tame his

Wooden instructs his players during the 1972 national championship game against Florida State University.

rebelliousness. But no punishment was meted out from the athletic department, on grounds that Walton's action came during the off season.

That was not the first or last headache the Academic All-American caused Wooden. Earlier that sophomore season, Walton had become increasingly surly, even rude to reporters. He had snapped at fans, too, especially if he thought they were infringing on his privacy. His popularity fell further that spring when he refused to try out for the U.S. Olympic team. He cited his sore knees as the reason, but his stance stirred memories of Alcindor's 1968 boycott. The U.S. team lost that summer to the Soviet Union in a controversial finish, marking the first time America failed to bring home a gold medal in basketball—and further souring people on Walton for his refusal to compete.

In the fall of 1972 Walton kept up his personal protest, showing up for the first day's practice with long, floppy hair. He had done so the year before and he would do so the following year. As always, Walton insisted that he had a right to wear his hair long and Wooden, as always, reminded his center that the coach had the right to choose UCLA's team. "Bill would think about it for a moment," recalled Wooden, "then get on his bicycle and pedal down to the Westwood barbershop for a trim." Walton, meanwhile, admitted to testing his coach but also respecting Wooden too much to cross him: "What was great about him, he never let you forget he was the boss."

In December 1972, three games into the new season, Wooden had his own unforgettable experience. He awoke in the early morning hours of December 11 suffering from a mild heart attack and was admitted to a Santa Monica hospital, where he spent the next week recovering. In more than thirty years of coaching, he

Wooden watches his UCLA team during a 1971 game. Although Wooden was criticized by opposing coaches and players for "riding the refs," his court conduct was usually reserved.

had never missed a game. When UCLA played the University of California, Santa Barbara, on December 16, he sat impatiently in his hospital bed as Cunningham directed the team. The outcome pleased him, a 98–67 Bruin victory. So did a visitor when he returned home. "When I opened the door, there stood that big, lovable redhead, Bill Walton," Wooden recalled. "He had come [ten miles] from the campus to the house on his bike just to see me in person. . . . That perked me up about as much as anything could have."

On returning home, Wooden also had time to read the December 25 issue of *Sports Illustrated*. His photo and that of tennis star Billie Jean King graced the cover, the magazine having named them "Sportsman and Sportswoman of 1972." Within months, Wooden would receive another major award—induction into the Naismith Memorial Basketball Hall of Fame as a coach, becoming the first to enter as both player *and* coach.

But more than honors were on his mind when Wooden resumed his place courtside after a one-game absence. UCLA's winning streak remained intact that winter, and soon the Bruins, who had not lost a game in nearly two years, were closing in on the record of sixty straight wins set in 1956 by Bill Russell's University of San Francisco team. The Bruins eventually reached the magic number on January 25, 1973, when they defeated Loyola University in Chicago Stadium. Two days later, they squared off against the University of Notre Dame in South Bend, Indiana. The Irish were the last team to have beaten the Bruins, back in January 1971, and Notre Dame was eager to be the spoiler again. But the Irish succumbed 82–63, and UCLA walked away with historic victory number sixty-one. After that, the wins kept coming, right into the NCAA tournament.

Wooden consults a program before a 1973 game against Loyola University. When someone once asked him why it took him so long to win a national championship, Wooden responded: "I'm a slow learner; but you notice when I learn something, I have it down pretty good."

The Bruins advanced easily to the Final Four in Saint Louis. There, in the Saturday semifinal, nostalgia mixed with anticipation as Wooden pitted his Number One-ranked team against Indiana University. Coached by thirty-two-year-old Bobby Knight, the Hoosiers had not made it past the opening round of the NCAA playoffs in twenty years, and oddsmakers gave the Hoosiers little chance of an upset. Although IU played well at the start, at halftime UCLA led 40–22.

When action resumed before the sellout crowd of 19,000, the Bruins proceeded to relax their press, lose their poise, force shots and, as a *Sports Illustrated* writer put it, exhibit "some of the worst basketball any UCLA team has played since before the pompon was invented." Pouncing, the Hoosiers scored seventeen straight points to narrow the Bruins' lead to 54–51 with more than nine minutes left on the clock. Leading the Hoosiers' comeback was husky center Steve Downing, who at that point had three fouls to Walton's four.

As play intensified, Walton collided with Downing and a controversial call followed. The referee assigned a fourth foul to Downing, rather than a fifth and final foul to Walton. Within a minute, Downing fouled again and was out of the game. The momentum having shifted, UCLA pulled away for a 70–59 victory. Asked after the game what might have happened had Walton fouled out and Downing continued playing, Wooden said his team would have won anyway. Knight, writing about the game years later, saw things differently: "I've always considered that fourth foul on Downing one of the two worst big calls my teams have ever had."

In the championship against Memphis State University, Walton again got into foul trouble. But having been outscored 26–14 by IU's Downing in the semifinal, Walton seemed determined to prove he was one of the college game's all-time greats. In a commanding offensive performance against Coach Gene Bartow's Tigers, Walton made twenty-one of twenty-two shots and scored forty-four points to lead the Bruins to an 87–66 win and their seventh straight NCAA championship. The victory closed out another 30–0 season for the Bruins—making them the only men's college team in history with back-to-back *undefeated* seasons—and extended their winning streak to seventy-five games. Walton also made it official: He would return for his senior year rather than turn pro.

Treated as a celebrity throughout the tournament weekend, Wooden found himself occupied with more than coaching. Increasingly called the "Wizard of Westwood," a title he disdained because he did not believe in wizardry, he was introduced to assistant coaches eager to shake his hand, chased after by the media, and asked to sign copies of *They Call Me Coach*, his newly published autobiography, on which he had collaborated with sportswriter Jack Tobin. Filled with stories of his youth and his philosophy on coaching and on life, the book was instantly popular and would remain so, eventually being updated and reissued. In 2002 *Sports Illustrated*'s editors listed it as one of the top one hundred sports books of all time.

Meanwhile, as fans and teams departed Saint Louis in March 1973, coaches continued a conversation steadily growing louder: Was UCLA's run of championships ruining the NCAA tournament? Was it good for college basketball in general to have a team win nine national titles in a single decade?

Oklahoma City University coach Abe Lemons did not weigh in publicly on those questions. But Lemons, famous for his homespun wit, summarized what many observers undoubtedly thought as the all-conquering 1973 Bruins took down Memphis State, and then took home their trophy: "Just another UCLA bullfight. You gore the matador all night. In the end he sticks it in you and the donkeys come on and drag you out."

16

"Be more concerned with your character than with your reputation.
Your character is what you really are while your reputation
is merely what others think you are."

John Wooden knew the 1973–74 basketball season would
be difficult. He had predicted as much two years earlier when,
following the Walton Gang's undefeated sophomore season, he had
gathered players in the locker room and told them they would be
an even better squad in their junior year, based on experience and
maturity. "But by the time you are seniors, you'll very likely become
intolerable," he had warned, leaving them to ponder his words.

Now that the "senior year" had at last arrived, Wooden himself
had plenty to ponder—not all of it to his liking. Throughout his
career he had conducted himself so as to command respect from
his players, and he had steered clear of trying to become a "buddy."
His purpose was to teach, his guiding principle fairness. As Wooden
once commented to a sportswriter, "A player gets the treatment he
earns and deserves."

But where Wooden exercised restraint in his personal dealings
with team members, a UCLA booster with no official ties to the
basketball program did not. Sam Gilbert, or "Papa G" as some
called him, was a wealthy Los Angeles contractor who made it
his business to cultivate a close rapport with certain players and,
with increasing regularity in the 1970s, Gilbert's association with

Businessman Sam Gilbert was a well-known figure among UCLA baskeball players during the 1960s and 1970s.

players grew. A few years younger than Wooden, Gilbert fostered Bruin friendships by regularly hosting gatherings at his Pacific Palisades home. He and his wife, Rose, invited players to spend Sundays there—to eat bagels, lounge by the pool, wash their cars, watch Sam barbecue steaks, and help themselves to whatever was in the refrigerator. Rose, a high school English teacher, would tutor them if requested. Sam, who had attended UCLA but never graduated, listened to their problems, doled out advice, and expounded on topics ranging from politics to sex.

Papa G and Mama G, as Rose was called, welcomed players during the holidays, too. The previous Thanksgiving, during Bill Walton's junior year, the Bruin center had enjoyed a turkey dinner there and then proven to player Andre McCarter, another attendee, that he could eat a whole pumpkin pie slathered with a quart of ice cream. For Christmas that same year, players Larry Farmer and Larry Hollyfield had presented the Gilberts, who owned twin Mercedes, with a Rolls-Royce—not the car, but a transistor radio popular at the time.

Gilbert's association with the team began during the Lew Alcindor era. Before 1966 he was said to be only a fan, occasionally dispensing apples and oranges to players after games. But that year, amid rumblings that Alcindor and Lucius Allen were thinking about transferring, former UCLA player Willie Naulls introduced the disgruntled sophomores to Gilbert for counseling. Gilbert became a confidant of the two young men, and soon other teammates were heading to Papa G's seaside home or to his Lake Arrowhead retreat for parties and relaxation.

Gilbert did not hide his ties to Bruin players. As Alcindor prepared to graduate in 1969, Gilbert openly helped the

"In the end," said Wooden, seen here during a 1973 game, "it's about the teaching, and what I always loved about coaching was the practices. Not the games, not the tournaments, not the alumni stuff. But teaching the players during practice was what coaching was all about to me."

superstar negotiate a $1.4 million, five-year contract with the Milwaukee Bucks. Gilbert continued to serve as "financial advisor," helping negotiate contracts for successive Bruin graduates such as Sidney Wicks, Curtis Rowe, Steve Patterson, and Henry Bibby—all at no charge.

Neither did the Gilberts keep the Sunday and holiday get-togethers a secret. In early 1973, in a wide-ranging article about the team, *Sports Illustrated* referenced the couple's hospitality and their "storybook house . . . occupied by antiques from all over the world." Three years earlier, in 1970, Gilbert made his chumminess with the team known in another way. After UCLA players sent President Richard Nixon their letter condemning the Vietnam War, Gilbert complained to the *Los Angeles Times* about the newspaper's failure to print the entire letter, and then offered the full text to a reporter.

It was against this backdrop that Wooden assembled the Bruins for the 1973–74 season. Years later, much more would become public about the nature and extent of Gilbert's "help," and Wooden would be criticized for not stopping players from accepting Gilbert's favors, which included his buying their basketball tickets at inflated prices and helping them get huge discounts on everything from clothes to stereos to cars. But early on, Wooden remained tight-lipped about Gilbert. He broke his silence long enough to tell sportswriters Dwight Chapin and Jeff Prugh, for their 1973 book *The Wizard of Westwood*: "I personally hardly know Sam Gilbert. . . . I think he's a person who's trying to be helpful in every way that he can. I sometimes feel that in his interest to be helpful it's in direct contrast with what I would like to have him do to be helpful."

Based on additional research for their book, Chapin and Prugh told of a "chasm" between the two men. "Privately," the *Westwood* authors wrote, "it is known that [Wooden and Gilbert] are sharply at odds over relating to players—a delicate issue within the UCLA basketball program. One view is that Gilbert 'interferes' . . . while another is that Wooden gets low marks from Gilbert for 'ignoring' the players as persons."

Virtually impossible to ignore, as the season got under way, was the team's winning streak. It stood at seventy-five games, and few expected the victory run to end anytime soon. UCLA quickly tacked on win number seventy-six in its season opener in late November. But the next night in Pauley Pavilion, where UCLA had not lost a game in almost four years, the Bruins were sorely tested by the University of Maryland. Coached by Lefty Driesell and led by heralded players John Lucas, Len Elmore, and Tom McMillen, the powerhouse East Coast squad came within a point, 65–64, of pulling off a stunning upset. "It ain't got a W after it, but I sure am proud," Driesell said afterward, thrilled that his team had almost stopped the streak.

Twelve games later, on January 19, 1974, UCLA faced another major test. The Bruins squared off in South Bend against the Number Two-ranked and undefeated University of Notre Dame, whose fans still savored the fact that the Irish were the last team to beat the Bruins before the streak—now up to eighty-eight games—had been launched in late January 1971. Pregame excitement ran so high that during practice that week Notre Dame coach Digger Phelps had his players cut down the nets in a rehearsal for victory.

Bruin fans, meanwhile, nursed pregame worries. Roughly two weeks earlier, Walton injured his back playing against Washington

State University and missed the next three games. His pain was so bad he could not get out of bed, and it remained questionable as to whether he would even make the trip east. But on game day, Walton took to the floor wearing a back brace and proceeded to make twelve of his first thirteen shots.

UCLA led 43–34 at the half, and with about three minutes left in the game, the Bruins were up by eleven points and seemingly well on their way to victory number eighty-nine. But suddenly, instead of looking invincible, UCLA committed four turnovers, missed easy tip-ins, and allowed Notre Dame to sink six straight shots, including a decisive jumper from Dwight "Iceman" Clay, to give the Irish a 71–70 win. The long victory streak had ended. For Walton and other members of "The Gang," it was their first loss ever in a Bruin uniform.

COURTESY UNIVERSITY OF NOTRE DAME ARCHIVES

Held aloft by ecstatic fans, University of Notre Dame players Adrian Dantley (left) and Ray "Dice" Martin cut down the nets following their team's ending of UCLA's eighty-eight-game winning streak on January 19, 1974.

Wooden accepted the defeat, and broken streak, with his characteristic calm. Years later, he admitted to having been "increasingly anxious" the previous season about breaking the University of San Francisco's sixty-game record, but "to be honest, once the Bruins set the record of 61 straight wins, extending it for its own sake was meaningless to me." His daughter Nan, who attended almost all the games during the streak, recalled her father suddenly feeling unburdened: "The only thing my dad ever said about it was that it was a relief when it was over. That's the way he felt. . . . It was like, 'It's OK. We'll start it all over again.'"

Six days later, the streak began anew when the Bruins romped over Santa Clara University by forty-two points and then, in a welcomed rematch, walloped Notre Dame by nineteen points at Pauley Pavilion. UCLA regained its Number One ranking. But just as quickly the Bruins suffered back-to-back losses against the University of Oregon and Oregon State University, prompting Wooden to publicly voice his displeasure. "We're certainly not No. 1," he told reporters. "Not the way we're playing. I wasn't concerned about it last week. I am now."

His concern sprang from the lack of on-court discipline, and to a degree he blamed himself. He had accommodated the off-court lifestyle and behavior of the Walton Gang more than he had that of past teams. Starting in the Alcindor era, Wooden had begun relaxing certain rules. He did not enforce curfew as strictly on road trips (trainer Ducky Drake did fewer bed checks) and he permitted players to grow their hair slightly longer. By the fall of 1970 he had begun tolerating longer sideburns, though he still forbade players to have beards and mustaches, and he had permitted more casual dress on road trips, no longer requiring the traditional navy blazers.

But those accommodations were not enough to satisfy the current crop of Bruins, and Wooden—partly because the team had amassed a flawless record the past two years—had accepted a "looseness" he previously would never have permitted. When Walton introduced his teammates to Transcendental Meditation, Wooden had allowed the players to use his office for meditating sessions. As players pronounced themselves "vegetarians," Wooden had relinquished his strict control of team meals. Moreover, in a rare break from his insistence on decorum, Wooden had permitted Walton to eat in his underwear at training table, so that the redhead could ice his knees.

By the end of 1973–74 regular season, Wooden managed to get his team refocused enough to win the conference title, advance out of the NCAA tournament regionals, and earn a berth in the Final Four in Greensboro, North Carolina. The Bruins' earlier missteps sent them into the tournament ranked second in the nation behind the Wolfpack of North Carolina State University, the very team that UCLA was set to play in the semifinal. Bruin players were not particularly worried. They had beaten NC State by eighteen points earlier in the year. The Wolfpack, meanwhile, had legitimate reasons to worry about their star player, David Thompson. During the previous week's regional game, he had crashed to the floor, been wheeled out on a stretcher, and received fifteen stitches in his scalp—stitches he still wore as the Bruin-Wolfpack rematch commenced.

Neither team dominated initially and, as leads were squandered and comebacks made, the game had all the makings of a nail-biter. Thompson's high-flying leaps—vertical jumps that earned him the nickname "Skywalker"—added to the excitement

and tension. At the buzzer, the game was tied. At the end of the
first overtime, another tie.

UCLA grabbed a seven-point lead in the second overtime and
finally looked ready to deliver the win. But just as quickly, NC
State whittled the lead down to one, Thompson hit a jumper, and
the Wolfpack went ahead 76–75. With the clock ticking down, the
Bruins bungled some last-attempt chances. The final score was 80–
77, a victory that sent NC State to the championship game, where it
beat Marquette University two nights later for the 1974 crown.

UCLA's loss sent shockwaves throughout the world of college
basketball. For the first time in eight years, the Bruins had not
advanced to the finals and would not bring home a trophy. On the
eve of the Final Four, a *Sports Illustrated* writer had asked: "Is there
anyone out there man enough, big and bad enough, to throw UCLA
off the mountain?" NC State had proven it was up to the task, and
UCLA's "reign of terror," as some coaches viewed Wooden's dynasty,
had ended.

Wooden admitted to being disappointed. But as he wrote years
later, his disappointment was with the *entire* season. Winning had
become routine for the Bruins, and his players, in his estimation,
stopped striving to get better: "Effort. Effort. Effort. That's the
highest and truest standard, and somehow it was compromised in
the 1974 season." He faulted himself for not having been "smart
enough" to prevent his team from growing complacent and for not
teaching his Bruins "to have a greater love for the effort than the
score." Late into his life, the answers still eluded him: "Here I am
many, many years later still wondering what I should have done."

17

"The main ingredient of stardom is the rest of the team."

Contrary to speculation in the media and elsewhere, John Wooden did not retire at the end of the 1973–74 season. Nell had earlier fueled talk about her husband's retirement when she told Dwight Chapin and Jeff Prugh for their 1973 book *The Wizard of Westwood*: "I've never asked him to get out of coaching, but I think he's about ready." Nell had added that the Wooden children, Nan and Jim, also hoped their father would call it quits soon: "These last few years haven't been the happiest of our lives. Fans are so greedy. They're dissatisfied if we win a championship game by only five points. That's why his children want him to get out."

Wooden's health had also led people to wonder when he might step aside. Although he had recovered from his heart attack, he had been ordered by his doctors to slow down and watch his diet. Some observers had begun speaking privately about how he looked tired and seemed to have aged rapidly. Wooden, however, professed to feel fit. He had given up smoking years earlier (when he did smoke, he always quit prior to the start of basketball season and resumed the habit only at season's end, so as not to violate his team "no-smoking" rule). Since his heart attack, he had also adopted an exercise regimen, walking five miles around UCLA's track early each morning. Still, in the spring of 1974, he was within months of turning sixty-four. Looming was UCLA's

mandatory requirement age of sixty-five—a requirement the
university could have waived for him until he turned sixty-seven.

Another factor feeding all the retirement speculation that spring
was Bill Walton's graduation. Walton's departure signaled the end
of an era in UCLA basketball, much like Lew Alcindor's leaving had
done, and people had surmised Wooden might exit with his three-
time collegiate Player of the Year. Talented members of the Walton
Gang—Keith Wilkes, Greg Lee, and Tommy Curtis—also graduated
that spring. That left the Bruins with only one starter, David Meyers,
to return in the fall, and no superstars loomed on the horizon.

In short order, however, Wooden put all the speculation to rest.
His love of the game and competitive spirit convinced him to return
for the 1974–75 season. He knew that replacing the previous year's
seniors would be difficult, but he looked forward to the challenge of
molding a new team. He also felt some relief, sensing, correctly, that
the rebels were gone. As sophomore Marques Johnson later put it:
"[Wooden] seemed a lot more relaxed . . . like, 'This is a group I can
control. I don't have any wild cards out there that I can't predict
what they're going to do.'"

The departure of Walton, the wildest of the wild cards, coincided
that summer with another leave-taking. President Richard Nixon
resigned in August 1974, facing almost certain impeachment for
his involvement in Watergate, the biggest political scandal in U.S.
history. Interestingly, though perhaps not surprisingly given the
turbulent times, the lives of Wooden, Walton, and Nixon had
intersected on more than one occasion in the preceding years.
Nixon's Vietnam War policies had sparked the antiwar protests in
which Walton participated, and for which he was jailed. Openly
critical of the nation's chief executive, Walton had routinely answered

his phone in college by saying "Impeach the President," and at one point he even wrote Nixon a letter accusing him of crimes against humanity. The Bruins' counterculture center sent the letter on UCLA basketball stationery, signed by him and his teammates.

Wooden had pleaded with Walton not to mail that letter, just as he had asked members of the 1970 Bruins squad not to send Nixon their missive. Those letters stood in sharp contrast to the telephone call Wooden had received from Nixon in 1970, congratulating the team on its most recent championship. Two years later, after the Walton Gang had helped UCLA secure another championship, Nixon had written Wooden to again extend his congratulations. That letter, which Wooden framed and hung in his home, read in part: "And you may be certain I am counted among those who think John Wooden is just about the finest coach in the long, exciting history of the game." The president sent Wooden two more letters the following season.

Nixon's White House Chief of Staff, H. R. "Bob" Haldeman, also shared a tie-in to this oddly connected trio. Graduating from UCLA in 1948, the year Wooden arrived, Haldeman had been an ardent basketball booster and eventually chaired the fund-raising drive for Pauley Pavilion, allowing him and Wooden to become better acquainted. Haldeman's political career, like that of Nixon's, was cut short by the Watergate scandal, and Haldeman was eventually convicted and sentenced to a federal prison north of Los Angeles for his role in the Watergate cover-up. While in prison, the disgraced Nixon aide received a visit from Wooden and Nell—a visit Haldeman never forgot. "That says something about his loyalty," said Haldeman, who was released on parole in 1978. "He came up to the prison visiting area and we chatted about baseball and

H. R. "Bob" Haldeman sits at his desk down the hall from the Oval Office in the White House, March 1973.

world conditions or whatever came to mind. His visiting me . . . was something that there was absolutely no need for him to do. . . . I think it's about as clear a picture of John Wooden as you can come up with."

Wooden, meanwhile, had more than politics to contend with as the 1974–75 season got under way. He named senior forward David Meyers captain for the entire season, contrary to his past practice of appointing captains from game to game. Nicknamed "Spider" for his rebound-grabbing arms, Meyers possessed an inner fire that Wooden could relate to: "David reminded me of my own style when I was at Purdue; he dove after loose balls, fought for everything, and played with a zeal that affected the whole team."

Joining Meyers as frontline starters were sophomores Johnson and Richard Washington. Starting at the guard positions were junior Andre McCarter and senior Pete Trgovich, both of whom

Wooden had deployed only sparingly in the past. Sharing Wooden's Hoosier roots, Trgovich had helped his East Chicago High School team win the 1971 Indiana state basketball championship. Years later, Trgovich returned to Indiana to coach a high school team to the 2007 state championship, though the team would be East Chicago Central, not his alma mater of East Chicago Washington.

Although newly constituted, the Bruins started the season solidly, rattling off twelve straight wins before losing two contests in January. They strung together more wins before getting thrashed by twenty-two points—one of the worst defeats in Wooden's entire coaching career—by the University of Washington. Still, at season's end, UCLA's 23–3 record was good enough to include a conference title and a return trip to the NCAA tournament, which had recently expanded to include thirty-two teams.

The Bruins scrapped and battled their way to the Final Four, prevailing even as other more touted teams stumbled en route. Among the fallen was Bobby Knight's Number One-ranked Indiana University, knocked off in the Mideast Regionals by the University of Kentucky Wildcats. Upon arriving in San Diego for the semifinals, UCLA prepared to go up against the University of Louisville, which meant another face-off between Wooden and his former assistant Denny Crum. The game also featured another reunion: UCLA's Trgovich and Louisville's star player, Ulysses "Junior" Bridgeman, had been high school teammates in East Chicago.

Intensely fought from the outset, the game quickly delivered on the high drama it promised. Louisville ran up nine-point leads four different times, but the Bruins kept charging back and even with forty-eight seconds left and trailing by four points, they tied the score and sent the game to overtime. Though a semifinal overtime had been UCLA's downfall a year earlier against North Carolina State University, the Bruins kept their cool. "Nobody was thinking back," UCLA captain Meyers said later. "It was time for bread and butter."

As the battle continued, Louisville pulled ahead 74–73. With twenty seconds left, UCLA fouled, sending Louisville guard Terry Howard to the line, where he could have sealed the victory by making both shots. But he missed the first of the one and one, allowing the Bruins to grab the ball and Wooden a chance to set up a last-second play. He assigned the closing shot to Washington, who arched it perfectly to give the Bruins a one-point lead. Louisville attempted a closing desperation shot, but the game was over. UCLA had earned the right to return to the championship game.

But more was over that Saturday than just a semifinal thriller. As Wooden embraced Crum, shook the hands of well-wishers, and made his way through the mob of exuberant fans, he felt, in his words, "almost ill, but I wasn't sick." Instead of heading to the press room, where reporters awaited him for a postgame interview, he veered into the locker room. A few players halted their celebrating long enough to pull up a chair for him to stand on, and the room gradually grew quiet as he offered the team his congratulations. Then came the jolt: "I'm bowing out." Monday night's championship game, he informed the stunned Bruins, would be his last.

Speculation about Wooden's retirement had not abated during the year, and months before the tournament Wooden had confided to a few people, UCLA athletic director J. D. Morgan among them, that he would leave at season's end. Rumors about his impending departure had intensified during the playoffs, and on the morning of the semifinal game both the *Los Angeles Times* and the *Los Angeles Herald Examiner* had reported that his retirement appeared

A rare moment of emotion on the bench for Wooden during the 1975 NCAA tournament. As a coach, Wooden believed that if a player did not do what he should in the game, the bench was the best place for him. "He'll come around," he noted.

imminent. Still, Wooden had remained publicly tight-lipped about his plans, and no one—not Nell nor his children nor Morgan— knew he planned to break the news that night. As he tried to explain later, "I don't know exactly why, but something in my head just said, 'It's over.'"

But he still had one more game to go, against the University of Kentucky for the championship. The Monday night contest pitted the Wildcats' hulking size against UCLA's quickness and speed. From the outset the pace was furious, with the lead changing fifteen times in the first half. When Wooden, using only his five starters and substitute center Ralph Drollinger, sent the Bruins back for second-half action, play remained intense. Eventually, however, the boys from Westwood pulled off a 92–85 win, giving

UCLA its tenth national championship in twelve years and allowing Wooden's coaching career to end on a triumphant note. The crowd of 15,000 gave him a four-minute standing ovation.

"I'm going to try and keep busy, occupied, and hope I have enough things so I won't go stale," Wooden said at his final tournament press conference. "I won't coach again, ever, but I always hope to be involved in some way with basketball." Still processing news that had finally become official, Morgan could not leave it at that: "It's the end of the active coaching career of the greatest college coach of all time."

Taking a shot before a UCLA game, Wooden displays the form that made him an All-American at Purdue. He once said that to be honest he did not believe he was "a fine game coach," but instead was a "good practice coach."

18

"You can't live a perfect day without doing something
for someone who will never be able to repay you."

If John Wooden had hoped to slip quietly into retirement, UCLA officials had other plans. The following October 14, which was also the day he turned sixty-five, the university threw Wooden a birthday/retirement party in Pauley Pavilion. Attended by nearly 7,000 well-wishers, the "Wooden Night" party featured speakers and celebrities ranging from entertainer Bob Hope to Los Angeles mayor Tom Bradley. The evening was filled with sentiment-laced tributes, repeated standing ovations, a rendition of "Auld Lang Syne," and retirement gifts, among them a Bruin blue Mercedes-Benz automobile.

In the months leading up to the party, UCLA's new basketball coach, Gene Bartow, had asked Wooden to remain on campus and even share an office. Bartow, whose Memphis State University Tigers lost to UCLA in the 1973 national championship game, wanted to pick the brain of his predecessor. "Several times we sat down and worked at the blackboard, actually using Xs and Os," said Bartow, who also quizzed Wooden on the zone press and the strengths of the returning Bruins.

But transitioning from one coach to another was awkward, and Wooden later faulted himself for not leaving sooner. "I should have realized my presence made him uncomfortable," Wooden told a reporter. When UCLA's first practice of the 1975–76 season began, the day after the party, Wooden and Nell set off on an eighteen-day Caribbean cruise, signaling that the transition was over. To Bartow and succeeding Bruin coaches, Wooden offered encouragement but avoided meddling. He contented himself with the role of spectator, rooting for the Bruins with Nell from seats behind the home bench at Pauley Pavilion.

Retirement did not mean idleness, however. Wooden occasionally served as a color commentator for televised UCLA games. He continued to speak at coaching clinics across the country. And he remained a teacher, instructing youths at summer basketball camps and, for a brief period in the 1980s, putting adults through workouts at weekend "fantasy" camps.

Teaching basketball in the off season was nothing new to Wooden. Starting in the 1960s he had organized and run day clinics at Pacific Palisades High School in Los Angeles. Ever popular, his clinics evolved into weeklong residential camps on the campus of California Lutheran College, located northwest of the city. The hundreds of roundball hopefuls who attended over the years received copies of Wooden's "Pyramid of Success" chart, listened to him preach the game's fundamentals, and practiced drills while he offered tips and advice. Many returned year after year, taking home, among other things, a photograph of the camper seated next to "Coach."

During the 1960s and 1970s Wooden also taught at Campbell College Basketball School, a summer camp in Buies Creek, North Carolina, known for attracting prominent instructors. In 1968 eleven-year-old Lendy Pridgen, a diehard University of North Carolina Tar Heel fan, met Wooden there. The young camper did not abandon his loyalty to the Tar Heels that summer, but he left Buies

Two of Wooden's finest players, Kareem Abdul-Jabbar (left) and Bill Walton, stand by their coach during a jersey retiring ceremony at Pauley Pavilion in Los Angeles, February 3, 1990.

Creek with a high regard for UCLA's coach, who he remembered as an "extremely patient man" and "very generous with his time." Pridgen, who years later became a health association executive in the Washington, D.C., area, retained another memory of Wooden: "Boy, did he work us hard." Campbell College, meanwhile, awarded Wooden an honorary doctor of humanities degree in 1973—the first such honorary degree that Wooden, having been offered others, chose to accept.

It was not only to highly touted camps that Wooden took his passion for teaching. In 1972 he conducted a weeklong clinic in Kendallville, Indiana, at the request of East Noble High School coach Jim Calvin, a Wooden acquaintance. Targeted to youth in the East Noble school district, Calvin recalled getting "phone calls every day that week from people all over the state wanting their kids to come." Wooden made enough of an impression that summer on young camper Hal Hossinger that decades later Hossinger, taking what he called "the world's longest long-shot," wrote Wooden and asked if he could visit him in Los Angeles. Wooden said yes, and in the summer of 2000 a much-older Hossinger reconnected with his much-older camp instructor. "It was just like going to talk to your Indiana grandfather," Hossinger recalled.

While Wooden shunned the limelight in his early years of retirement, he found himself thrust into the news in the early 1980s. In December 1981, six years after he left coaching and after UCLA had already gone through three head coaches (Larry Farmer was at that point the fourth), the NCAA placed UCLA's basketball team on a two-year probation for rules violations, some involving team booster Sam Gilbert. Among the violations was Gilbert's cosigning of a promissory note that allowed a player to buy a car.

The NCAA took no legal action against Gilbert, but ordered the
school to distance itself from him. None of the violations were linked
to Wooden's era.

Soon after the NCAA's ruling, however, the *Los Angeles Times*
published articles alleging that Gilbert had provided illegal gifts and
services to Bruin players for fifteen years, including during Wooden's
tenure. The *Times*'s series also said Gilbert offered enticements
to recruit players, though those offers occurred in the years *after*
Wooden retired. "Each coach has dealt with Gilbert in his own way.
. . . Wooden said he was never particularly concerned about Gilbert
and had no reason to believe Gilbert was breaking any rules," the
newspaper reported in early 1982. The *Times* also quoted Wooden as
saying: "Maybe I had tunnel vision. I still don't think he's [Gilbert]
had any great impact on the basketball program. . . . Maybe I trusted
too much."

In a follow-up interview with the *New York Times* in February
1982, Wooden said he knew his players went to Gilbert's home and
were close to him. "But you can't pick someone's friends," he said. "I
talked to the players and tried to make them aware of what was good
and bad, but I didn't try to run their lives."

In the years that followed, many people—coaches, sportswriters,
players, and others—speculated publicly on the Wooden-Gilbert
association. Some criticized Wooden for knowing about Papa Sam's
rules-bending actions and looking the other way. Others faulted
Wooden for not wanting to know, for deliberately choosing to be
uninformed. Aware of the criticism and ongoing debate, Wooden
consistently maintained that Gilbert did not corrupt UCLA's program
while he was coach. "I know I never used him," Wooden told the
Basketball Times in 2005, three decades after his retirement from the

game. "My conscience is clear."

Gilbert, meanwhile, remained an overzealous booster into the mid-1980s. In 1987, after UCLA turned Gilbert in for another recruiting violation, the NCAA took away two basketball scholarships and again ordered the university to sever all ties with him. In November of that year Gilbert died of cancer, just days before federal marshals, unaware of his death, showed up at his home intending to arrest him on charges of laundering money in a drug-smuggling scheme. Papa Sam was seventy-four.

* * * *

Starting in the early 1980s, Nell's health worried Wooden greatly. She suffered a heart attack while undergoing a hip replacement operation in 1982, putting her in a coma. Wooden spent ten- and twelve-hour days at her bedside, clasping her hand and talking to her in hopes that she might hear him. After three months, she slowly came out the coma and eventually returned home. Her health continued to fail, and she underwent more surgery to remove her gall bladder. But she battled and in spring 1984 she even managed to attend the NCAA Final Four—an event to which she had accompanied Wooden for more than thirty years. Sportswriter John Feinstein recalled seeing the Woodens in a Seattle hotel lobby, greeting old friends:

> One night, after all the greetings, Coach started pushing Nell [in her wheelchair] toward the elevator to go to bed. One person started to clap—and the next thing you know the entire lobby just sort of opened up a pathway and everyone gave the Woodens a standing ovation. It was one of the most powerful experiences I have ever had in sports. . . . There weren't too many dry eyes in the Hilton lobby that night.

Months later, on Christmas morning 1984, Nell was rushed to the hospital suffering from more ailments. She died on March 21, 1985, at age seventy-three. She and Wooden had been married for nearly fifty-three years and, as he liked to tell people, "sweethearts" for sixty years.

Nell's death left Wooden inconsolable. Family and friends worried about him, as did former players and assistant coaches, who made a point of telephoning him regularly. "I was desolate," he wrote later. "I became almost a recluse and didn't care to do anything or see anyone. This went on for months; it seemed like years." He was told by those closest to him that they feared for his life. "They may have been right," he said.

Wooden refused to move from the modest condominium in Encino, a Los Angeles neighborhood, where he and Nell had resided since 1973. He also refused to change anything in it, preferring to hold tight to memories recalled by Nell's robe, her choice of furniture, and how she had arranged the pictures. On the twenty-first of each month he started a tradition of writing her a love letter, which he placed on her pillow, the stack of letters neatly bound in a yellow ribbon growing taller by the year. Every Sunday he visited her grave.

Though never fully recovering from Nell's death, Wooden gradually emerged from his deep grief. Helping him recover were his great-grandchildren, the first one, Cori, born the year Nell died, with others quickly following, the number growing to thirteen. As he began making public appearances again, his calendar filled quickly. He attended charity events. He lectured from time to time in a UCLA classroom or to coaches and staff. He accepted invitations from corporations and organizations to give

Describing Wooden in a column, sportswriter Rick Reilly said there has "never been another coach like Wooden, quiet as an April snow and square as a game of checkers; loyal to one woman, one school, one way; walking around campus in his sensible shoes and Jimmy Stewart morals."

motivational speeches based on his Pyramid, often flying around the country to deliver them.

In the 1990s he also began writing and coauthoring books. Most were geared to adults, some to children. All were intended to be inspirational, filled with his homespun maxims ("Be quick, but don't hurry") and common-sense wisdom. As he wrote, he also continued to read—revisiting his favorite works of literature (from John Milton to William Cullen Bryant), enjoying poems he had read as a young man (especially Thomas Gray's "Elegy Written in a Country Churchyard"), and setting aside time daily for his Bible. A lifelong learner, he also boned up on Zen philosophy and studied the lives of Abraham Lincoln and Mother Teresa, greatly admiring both. He wrote poetry, too, his preferred form being rhyme.

Never seeking to get rich off his cachet-laden name, he loaned it to worthy causes. In 1994 an annual basketball tournament called the Wooden Classic was established to benefit one of his favorite charities, Special Olympics Southern California. Six years later, a similar tournament in Indianapolis—the John R. Wooden Tradition—began to benefit the Hoosier State's Special Olympics. Leadership programs and awards also made use of his name. UCLA's school of management introduced the John Wooden Global Leadership Award in 2008, a sign that his legacy rests as much on lessons imbedded in his Pyramid as on his basketball accomplishments. Recipients of that leadership award have included the CEOs of companies such as Starbucks, American Express, and Federal Express.

With each passing year, Wooden's name also began showing up on buildings—inside and out. As early as 1983 UCLA honored him when it opened the John R. Wooden Recreation and Sports Center.

In 2003 the basketball court inside Pauley Pavilion was named the Nell and John Wooden Court, with Wooden insisting that Nell's name come first. Indiana State University bestowed the same honor in 2008, naming its home court the Nellie and John Wooden Court.

In like manner, a Los Angeles school for at-risk youth was renamed John R. Wooden High School in 2005. And in 2006, on Wooden's ninety-sixth birthday, a post office in Reseda, California, was renamed the Coach John Wooden Post Office by an act of Congress. Wooden showed up for that occasion looking dapper in his traditional navy jacket, just as he had looked spry a year earlier when he recited three poems from memory at the high school renaming ceremony. "No cheat sheets, no nudge from

The Nell and John Wooden Court at UCLA's Pauley Pavilion.

Wooden shakes hands with President George W. Bush after receiving the Presidential Medal of Freedom during a ceremony at the White House on July 23, 2003. Established by President Harry S Truman, the medal is given annually to individuals of "significant public or private accomplishment" and for "recognized exceptional meritorious service."

dedicated daughter, Nan [Wooden], and yet every word delivered in a clear voice worthy of a prime-time radio gig," reported the *Los Angeles Times*.

Wooden's mental acuity remained sharp as his age inched toward one hundred. He renewed his driver's license at age ninety-five and continued driving around in his Ford Taurus. He gave talks and remained a mentor to younger generations. Among those he befriended was UCLA's women's gymnastics coach Valorie Kondos Field, who at one point in the mid-1990s had become so dispirited she considered leaving coaching. After reading one of his books, from which she drew inspiration, she invited Wooden to dinner and then to one of her practices. He soon formed a friendship with her team and became a regular at meets. "If we'd never met, I might not be coaching right now," said Kondos Field in 2008, crediting him with much of her eventual coaching success.

Basketball also remained part of Wooden's life, and into his mid-nineties he frequently attended UCLA's home basketball games. In his reserved Pauley Pavilion seat, he graciously posed for pictures and signed autographs nonstop before games and during halftime. "He must have signed a million autographs in his life because he never turned anyone down," said Bill Bennett, a UCLA athletics official who worked with Wooden in his postcoaching years. Meanwhile, many of his former players regularly stayed in touch, calling him on the phone, dropping by his condo, and driving him to appointments. At one point, Wooden could locate 172 of the 180 Bruins he had coached, and he was as pleased to meet with his former "subs" as he was to chat with his stars (more than two dozen of whom played in the National Basketball Association).

In late February 2008 Wooden fell in his condo, breaking his wrist and collarbone. His physical decline was pronounced after that; he was forced to trade his cane for a wheelchair, and bouts of pneumonia sent him to the hospital in 2009 and again in 2010. Even with those health setbacks, however, he maintained his sunny disposition. And whenever possible, he showed up for breakfast at VIP's, a neighborhood restaurant he had long patronized, accompanied by his grandchildren, former players, or his full-time caregiver, UCLA athletic trainer Tony Spino.

On May 26, 2010, Wooden was hospitalized again, this time due to dehydration. His family was with him at Ronald Reagan UCLA Medical Center, and in the coming days he was permitted some visitors, among them Bill Walton, Jamaal (formerly Keith) Wilkes, and Kareem Abdul-Jabbar, who had gone straight to the hospital upon taking a flight home from Europe. Around 6:45 p.m. on Friday, June 4, about three hours after Abdul-Jabbar's visit and as other friends huddled in the hospital waiting room, word came that Wooden had died. He was ninety-nine, exactly 132 days shy of his hundredth birthday, an occasion for which the university was already planning a party.

At 8:00 p.m., across the street from the medical center, hundreds of UCLA students gathered for a rally. They called out the name "Co-ach Woo-den" and followed it with the traditional Bruin eight-clap cheer. A moment of silence followed, with the students holding up candles. They dispersed quietly.

Epilogue

*"What you are as a person is far more important than
what you are as a basketball player."*

On June 26, 2010, two weeks after John Wooden was laid to
rest in a private ceremony in Hollywood Hills, his public funeral
took place in Pauley Pavilion. About 4,000 people—coaches,
former players, university colleagues, admirers from all walks
of life—attended the memorial service, at which Wooden was
eulogized for having been a humble and exceptionally decent man
who stayed true to his core values even as he showed flexibility.
"He was born when the automobile was just out of its infancy. . . .
And he lived to see men walk on the moon and to see computers
recast the world," said sportscaster Al Michaels, who opened the
ceremony. "But he was never resistant. He understood how to
shift with the times. . . . His life was built on an indestructible,
unshakeable foundation."

In the weeks and months after Wooden's death, more tributes
were paid and new ways were found to honor him. That autumn
his family donated his furnishings and personal items to UCLA,
which in turn created a Wooden exhibition. Today visitors to the
UCLA Athletic Hall of Fame can view a video of his life and see
his home den exactly as it appeared in his condominium—his
oversized recliner; his framed letters and photographs; and his
rolltop desk, where he began each morning opening mail, writing
poetry, and signing the dozens of basketballs and books sent to
him by fans. Wooden unfailingly returned the autographed items
to their owners, usually at his own expense.

Shelves at VIP's, the restaurant where Wooden regularly dined, are lined with mementos honoring the longtime UCLA coach.

In 2012 the homage-paying continued, this time with the unveiling of Wooden statues in Indianapolis and outside Pauley Pavilion. That November brought another tribute. In a nod to Wooden's roots as a college coach, UCLA invited Indiana State University to play in the basketball season opener, an event that also marked the grand reopening of a renovated Pauley Pavilion. The rejuvenated arena includes a walkway, called "Wooden Way," lined with display cabinets that tell his life story through artifacts and photos.

In less dramatic but still telling fashion, Wooden's memory is kept alive at VIP's, the restaurant where for roughly fifteen years he arrived at 8:30 a.m. daily, took his usual seat in a back booth, and ordered his breakfast of scrambled eggs and bacon. VIP's owner Paul Ma has placed a sign over the booth identifying it as Wooden's favorite, and the restaurant's walls and shelves remain filled with Wooden photographs and memorabilia—a shrine to a beloved customer. "Every day I saw Coach I felt I became a better person," said Ma, a native of China who read one of Wooden's books upon buying the restaurant in 1998 and who credits Wooden with having "really impacted me" on how to treat customers and manage a business. On the day of Wooden's public funeral, Ma closed the restaurant. He, like so many others, went to Pauley Pavilion to pay his respects.

Hoosiers also paid their respects that day. Martinsville native Jerry Sichting was at the memorial service, attending with his friend and former Boston Celtics teammate Bill Walton. When Sichting graduated from Martinsville High School in 1975, the year Wooden retired, he was awarded the school's first John R. Wooden Mental Attitude Award, which is still presented each spring to a deserving member of the boys' basketball team (Sichting received the award from Sam P. Alford, Martinsville High School's coach at the time and the father of Steve Alford, who became UCLA's head coach in the spring of 2013). Sichting, who starred at Purdue and played and coached in the National Basketball Association, had occasions over the years to meet Wooden, whom he greatly admired. As a boy growing up in Martinsville, Sichting also had another connection to the coaching legend: his grandmother, Verna McDaniel, attended high school with Wooden and, as Sichting recalled, "the old-timers were always talking about him."

In strictly basketball terms, Wooden's legacy can be grasped instantly by glancing toward the rafters in Pauley Pavilion, where eleven blue-and-gold banners representing UCLA's eleven national men's basketball titles hang. The last banner went up in 1995, when Jim Harrick was coach. The first ten came during Wooden's reign— that magical period from 1964 to 1975 when his teams mesmerized the nation and helped transform college basketball into the March Madness phenomenon of today. In the years leading up to and including those first ten NCAA championships, a span of twenty-seven years, Wooden compiled a 620–147 record as Bruins' coach, for a winning percentage of .808. What the banners and win-loss record do not show, but what Wooden was especially proud of, is that most of his lettermen between 1948 and 1975 graduated, either on time or eventually. He put the figure at "over 90 percent."

In becoming a coaching legend, Wooden did not let success spoil him or cause him to rest on his laurels. He had more to offer, and it was during his second career—this one lasting nearly thirty-five years—that his legacy grew. The famous teacher of hoops fundamentals and lessons in personal development became, in the last third of his life, the unassuming friend who shared of himself endlessly. He carved out time for those he knew well, those he barely knew, and complete strangers. Along the way, his generosity profoundly touched people.

UCLA Athletics official Bill Bennett recalled the morning he arrived extra early at his office because he wanted to call and wish Wooden a happy birthday. Bennett knew that two hundred to three hundred calls would be placed by 8:00 a.m. or 9:00 a.m., making it impossible to get through and overloading Wooden's voicemail machine. But before Bennett could place his early-morning call, he noticed that a voicemail message awaited him. When he hit the "play" button, Bennett heard Wooden singing "Happy Birthday." Bennett, like Wooden, was born on October 14. "Every morning for many, many years, I started every day listening to him sing 'Happy Birthday' to me," said Bennett, who keeps a copy of Wooden's Pyramid of Success on his office wall. When faced with a major decision, Bennett still asks himself, "What advice would Coach Wooden give me?"

For all his virtues, "Saint John"—as some had mockingly called Wooden during his coaching days—always admitted to having faults. He was never proud of the times when he yelled at opponents to "Quit crying" or called them "butcher." He was remorseful enough on at least one occasion to write to University of Notre Dame coach Digger Phelps and apologize for having complained during a game in South Bend about Irish center John Shumate: "Please convey my feeling to John. He is a fine

COURTESY INDIANAPOLIS STAR

Interviewed by the Indianapolis Star *when he was ninety-five, Wooden, asked about his greatest accomplishment, said, "The rapport and association I have with all my players is what I'm most proud of."*

young man . . . and I did him an injustice." As for needling referees through his rolled-up program, Wooden acknowledged as much, but had enough good sense to know when to stop. By his count, he received only two technical fouls during his entire coaching career, and his court conduct, if on occasions agitated, never gave way to histrionics. He was adamant that he never cursed: "Of course, I have told referees that I couldn't tell their tops from their bottoms, which is almost as bad as swearing."

Over the course of his long life, many savored his wit as much as his wisdom. His dry-humored remarks—delivered with a half grin and a twinkle in his blue eyes—often came out of nowhere, and he enjoyed poking fun at himself. He took particular pleasure in sharing an Elkhart, Indiana, newspaper clipping that referenced an event in 1946: "Johnny Wooden, South Bend Central's basketball coach, will be the featured speaker at Elkhart High's sports banquet, although they had hoped to line up some prominent coach." He retained his sense of humor to the very end, even as he lay in his hospital bed. To the visiting Bill Walton, the dying Wooden quipped, "I thought I was finished with you."

What Wooden never finished with, or more precisely, what he never stopped appreciating, was his Indiana upbringing. Martinsville remained special to him, and late into his life he returned there to meet old friends, drop by his former church, or stop by the new high school gym named for him in 1989. Always, too, he visited the cemetery in Centerton.

He cherished Indiana as the place that gave him his moral and intellectual footing. He remembered it as well for the place where he fell in love with the "beautiful . . . almost majestic" game of basketball, where he idolized an all-time great Hoosier player named Robert "Fuzzy" Vandivier, and where he tested and honed the coaching skills he took to UCLA. Indiana, too, is where Wooden landed in the record books for another sport. While playing golf in 1939 at Erskine Park Golf Course in South Bend, he had a hole in one and a double eagle in the same round, a feat that *Golf Digest* says only four other people have ever documented.

In California, Wooden's old-fashioned values and Midwest sensibilities, coupled with his prim, professorial bearing, made him a puzzling character. "John Wooden's so square he's divisible by four," *Los Angeles Times* columnist Jim Murray once famously said. But patiently, carefully, methodically, Wooden won over the hearts and minds of Bruin fans, and in time he won over much of the sporting universe.

"The tragedy of life is what dies inside a man while he lives," Vin Scully, Los Angeles Dodgers broadcaster and longtime friend, said via video at Wooden's memorial service. "The triumph of life is to be hopeful, kindly, cheerful, reverent and to keep the heart unwrinkled. The coach kept his heart unwrinkled. He was truly triumphant."

Learn More about John Wooden

Books

Abdul-Jabbar, Kareem. *Kareem*. With Mignon McCarty. New York: Random House, 1990.

Beck, Bill. *Play On: Celebrating 100 Years of High School Sports in Indiana*. Indianapolis: Cranfill and Company for the Indiana High School Athletic Association, 2003.

Bjarkman, Peter C. *The Biographical History of Basketball*. Chicago: Masters Press, 2000.

Chapin, Dwight, and Jeff Prugh. *The Wizard of Westwood: Coach John Wooden and His UCLA Bruins*. Boston: Houghton Mifflin Company, 1973.

Davis, Seth. *Wooden: A Coach's Life*. New York: Times Books/Henry Holt and Company, 2014.

Denny, Dick. *Glory Days Indiana: Legends of Indiana High School Basketball*. Champaign, IL: Sports Publishing, 2006.

Feinstein, John. *Last Dance: Behind the Scenes at the Final Four*. New York: Little, Brown and Company, 2006.

Gould, Todd. *Pioneers of the Hardwood: Indiana and the Birth of Professional Basketball*. Bloomington: Indiana University Press, 1998.

Graham, Tom, and Rachel Graham Cody. *Getting Open: The Unknown Story of Bill Garrett and the Integration of College Basketball*. New York: Atria Books/Simon and Schuster, 2006.

Halberstam, David. *The Breaks of the Game*. New York: Alfred A. Knopf, 1981.

Hammel, Bob. *Hoosiers Classified: Indiana's Love Affair with One-Class Basketball*. Indianapolis: Masters Press, 1997.

Heisler, Mark. *They Shoot Coaches, Don't They? UCLA and the NCAA Since John Wooden*. New York: Macmillan, 1996.

Hill, Andrew. *Be Quick—But Don't Hurry!* With John Wooden. New York: Simon and Schuster, 2001.

Hoffer, Richard. *Wooden: Basketball and Beyond: The Official UCLA Retrospective*. San Diego, CA: Skybox Press, 2011.

Hoose, Phillip M. *Hoosiers: The Fabulous Basketball Life of Indiana*. 1986. Reprint, Indianapolis: Guild Press of Indiana, 1995.

Johnson, Neville L. *The John Wooden Pyramid of Success*. Los Angeles: Cool Titles, 2000.

Katz, Milton S. *Breaking Through: John B. McLendon, Basketball Legend and Civil Rights Pioneer*. Fayetteville: University of Arkansas Press, 2007.

Knight, Bob. *Knight: My Story*. With Bob Hammel. New York: Saint Martin's Press, 2002.

Laskowski, John. *Tales from the Hoosier Locker Room*. With Stan Sutton. Champaign, IL: Sports Publishing, 2003.

MacCambridge, Michael, ed. *ESPN Sports Century*. New York: Hyperion, 1999.

Madison, James H. *A Lynching in the Heartland: Race and Memory in America*. New York: Saint Martin's Press, 2001.

Nater, Swen, and Ronald Gallimore. *You Haven't Taught Until They Have Learned: John Wooden's Teaching Principles and Practices*. Morgantown, WV: Fitness Information Technology, 2006.

Reger, John. *Quotable Wooden*. Lanham, MD: Taylor Trade Publishing, 2002.

Schwomeyer, Herb. *Hoosier Hysteria: A History of Indiana High School Boys Single Class Basketball*. 9th ed. Greenfield, IN: Mitchell-Fleming Printing, 1997.

Smith, John Matthew. *The Sons of Westwood: John Wooden, UCLA, and the Dynasty That Changed College Basketball*. Urbana: University of Illinois Press, 2013.

Walton, Bill. *Nothing but Net: Just Give Me the Ball and Get Out of the Way*. With Gene Wojciechowski. New York: Hyperion, 1994.

Williams, Pat. *Coach Wooden: The 7 Principles That Shaped His Life and Will Change Yours*. With Jim Denney. Grand Rapids, MI: Revell, 2011.

———. *How to Be Like Coach Wooden: Life Lessons from Basketball's Greatest Leader*. With David Wimbish. Deerfield Beach, FL: Health Communications, 2006.

Wooden, John R. *Practical Modern Basketball*. 3rd ed. Boston: Allyn and Bacon, 1999.

———. *They Call Me Coach*. With Jack Tobin. New York: McGraw-Hill, 2004.

———, and Steve Jamison. *Coach Wooden's Leadership Game Plan for Success: 12 Lessons for Extraordinary Performance and Personal Excellence*. New York: McGraw-Hill, 2009.

———. *My Personal Best: Life Lessons from an All-American Journey*. With Steve Jamison. New York: McGraw-Hill, 2004.

———, and Steve Jamison. *The Essential Wooden: A Lifetime of Lessons on Leaders and Leadership*. New York: McGraw-Hill, 2007.

———. *Wooden: A Lifetime of Observations and Reflections On and Off the Court*. With Steve Jamison. New York: McGraw-Hill, 1997.

———, and Steve Jamison. *The Wisdom of Wooden: My Century On and Off the Court*. New York: McGraw-Hill, 2010.

———, and Don Yaeger. *A Game Plan for Life: The Power of Mentoring*. New York: Bloomsbury, 2009.

Yaeger, Don. *Undue Process: The NCAA's Injustice for All*. Champaign, IL: Sagamore Publishing, 1991.

Magazine/Newspaper Articles

"A Lasting Moral Victory." *Indianapolis Star*, June 6, 2010.

"A Milestone Deserving of Permanent Commemoration." *Terre Haute Tribune-Star*, June 23, 2010.

Cave, Ray. "Wizards in the Land of Oz." *Sports Illustrated*, March 19, 1962.

DeFord, Frank. "The Team of '64." *Sports Illustrated*, March 26, 1979.

Deitsch, Richard. "Q & A: John Wooden." *Sports Illustrated*, March 31, 2003.

DeKever, Peter J. "On the Brink: Shelby Shake and Johnny Wooden." *Indiana Basketball History Magazine* (Summer 2005).

Greenberg, Steve. "John Wooden." *Sporting News Magazine*, January 5, 2009.

Jares, Joe. "The Two Faces of the Rubber Man." *Sports Illustrated*, January 6, 1969.

———. "Victory by Mystique." *Sports Illustrated*, March 30, 1970.

"John Wooden 1910–2010." *Basketball Times* (July 2010).

"John Wooden 1910–2010: Saying Goodbye to a Legend." *Indiana Basketball History Magazine* (Fall 2010).

"John Wooden: Coaching Legend." *Referee Magazine* (November 1999).

"John Wooden Built the Foundation for His Legacy at Indiana State Teacher's College." *Terre Haute Tribune-Star*, June 19, 2010.

Hyman, Mervin. "A Press That Panics Them All." *Sports Illustrated*, December 6, 1965.

Kirkpatrick, Curry. "UCLA: Simple, Awesomely Simple." *Sports Illustrated*, November, 30, 1970.

———. "Oh, Johnny, Oh, Johnny Oh!" *Sports Illustrated*, April 3, 1972.

———. "What a Wiz of a Win It Was." *Sports Illustrated*, April 7, 1975.

———. "Wise in the Ways of the Wizard." *Sports Illustrated*, November 30, 1981.

McCallum, Jack. "The March of the Wooden Soldiers." *Sports Illustrated*, April 16, 1984.

———. "At the Wooden Summer Camp, the Coach Was More Than a Stick Figure." *Sports Illustrated*, September 17, 1984.

McDermott, Barry. "After 88 Comes Zero." *Sports Illustrated,* January 28, 1974.

Meyer, Paula. "Standing Tall—Indiana State Remembers John Wooden." *Indiana State University Magazine* (September 2010).

Moses, Sam. "Pursued by a Very Long Shadow." *Sports Illustrated*, November 17, 1975.

Posnanski, Joe. "Color Wall Came Down Here in '48." *Kansas City Star*, March 13, 2002.

Reed, William F. "Court Trial for UCLA's New Gang." *Sports Illustrated*, January 10, 1972.

———. "Welcome to the Ball." *Sports Illustrated*, March 27, 1972.

"Remembering John Wooden." *Los Angeles Times*, June 13, 2010.

Soderburg, Wendy, ed. "We Will Always Call Him Coach." *UCLA Magazine* (October 2010).

"Sports' 50 Greatest Coaches." *Sporting News Magazine*, August 3, 2009.

Tomak, Curtis H., Joanne Raetz Stuttgen, and Norma J. Tomak. "John Wooden: A Revised Beginning, Part 1." *Connections: The Hoosier Genealogist* (Spring/Summer 2012); "Part 2." (Fall/Winter 2012).

Underwood, John. "Five Midgets and a Wink at Nell." *Sports Illustrated*, February 24, 1964.

Wind, Herbert Warren. "The Sporting Scene: West of the Wabash." *The New Yorker*, March 22, 1969.

Wolff, Alexander. "Call Him Irreplaceable." *Sports Illustrated*, April 11, 1988.

———. "The Coach and His Champion." *Sports Illustrated*, April 3, 1989.

———. "Birth of a Dynasty." *Sports Illustrated*, March 19, 2007.

———. "Remembering the Wizard." *Sports Illustrated*, June 14, 2010.

"Wooden Remembers Booster." *New York Times*, February 3, 1982.

Videos

Charlie Rose. Interview with John Wooden, aired December 15, 2000.

ESPN SportsCentury. Documentary on John Wooden, aired September 25, 2003.

John Wooden: The Indiana Story. Produced by the *Indianapolis Star*, 2010.

John Wooden: They Called Him Coach. Produced by Day of Discovery, 2013.

"NAIA Celebrates Black History Month—The Clarence Walker Story," http://www.youtube.com/watch?v=6TPw7UnCG3g.

Unpublished Source

Walker, Clarence. "Mr. J. C." Typewritten journal kept by Walker during his 1947–48 basketball season at Indiana State Teachers College. Copy provided by his son, Kevin Walker.

Websites

"A Timeline of John Wooden's Life," http://www.tinyurl.com/33uldb7.

 "An American Icon: John R. Wooden," http://www.uclabruins.com/coach-wooden.

John Wooden's Coaching Record at South Bend Central High School, http://etpearlstj2.homestead.com/central40s.html.

Indiana Basketball Hall of Fame, http://www.hoopshall.com/.

Naismith Memorial Basketball Hall of Fame, http://www.hoophall.com/.

The Official Site of Coach John Wooden, http://www.coachwooden.com/.

John Wooden's Coaching Record/Achievements

His coaching career spanned forty-three years (1932 to 1975); only two losing seasons.

Coached two years at Dayton High School in Dayton, Kentucky (21–14 record).

Coached at South Bend Central High School in South Bend, Indiana; head coach from 1936 to 1943, and after returning from military service, head coach in 1946, assuming job in midseason (148–49 record).

Coached two years at Indiana State Teachers College (44–15 record) and led the Sycamores to the finals of the 1948 NAIB tournament, losing to Louisville.

Coached twenty-seven years at UCLA (620–147 record).

Led Bruins to ten NCAA national championships in twelve years (1964–65, 1967–73, and 1975).

Led Bruins to seven straight NCAA national championships (1967 to 1973).

Led Bruins to thirty-eight straight NCAA tournament victories.

Led Bruins to eighty-eight consecutive victories.

Led Bruins to four 30–0 seasons.

First person inducted into the Naismith Memorial Basketball Hall of Fame both as a player (1960) and as a coach (1973).

Inducted into the inaugural class of the Indiana Basketball Hall of Fame (1962).

Inducted into the Indiana State University Athletics Hall of Fame (1984).

Inducted into the inaugural class of the Pac-10 Basketball Hall of Honor (2002).

Inducted into the National Collegiate Basketball Hall of Fame as a charter member (2006).

AP Coach of the Year five times: 1967, 1969, 1970, 1972, 1973.

UPI Coach of the Year six times: 1964, 1967, 1969, 1970, 1972, 1973.

Named "Sportsman of the Year" by *Sports Illustrated* (1972).

Received the NCAA's highest honor, the Theodore Roosevelt Award (1996).

Awarded the Presidential Medal of Freedom, the nation's highest civilian honor, by President George W. Bush (2003).

Named the "Greatest Coach" ever in any sport by *Sporting News* (2009).

Index